Slaves

with

SWAG

D1065942

Knowledge of Self Publishing, LLC
Permissions Department
P.O. Box 1010
California, Maryland 20619
info@knowledgeofselfpublishing.com
www.knowledgeofselfpublishing.com

ISBN-10:   0-9787862-1-1
ISBN-13:   978-0-9787862-1-2
Registered with the United States Library of Congress.
Includes cover, content, notes, bibliographical references and
index.

MONEY BACK GUARANTEE

The intent of this book is to provide not very well publicized historical facts as documented by past historians, intellectuals, professors, etc. The reader is strongly encouraged to read other texts that both agree with and oppose documented facts presented here to get the full picture of history.

This book is not offered as an all encompassing history book, but rather as a guide to offer the reader a different perspective of the History discipline. The author and the publishing house assume no responsibility and neither shall have any responsibility greater than the price of this book for any direct or indirect damage believed to have been caused by any information contained herein. Please feel free to contact the publisher for a full refund of the purchase price if you do not agree to be bound by the above disclaimer, otherwise your purchase constitutes agreement.

That being said, we at Knowledge of Self Publishing feel so certain that you will learn something new about history and/or get the opportunity to see history from a different perspective that we GUARANTEE it. It is unprecedented in the publishing industry to offer a MONEY BACK GUARANTEE on a book, but this is an unprecedented book. Therefore, here is our:

MONEY BACK GUARANTEE!

If after reading this text in its entirety you have not learned anything new and have not experienced a different perspective of history, contact the publisher for a full refund of the purchase price! *

*Only the ultimate consumer (reader) is eligible for the Money Back Guarantee. Contact Knowledge of Self Publishing for details.

This book is written in honor of my Father, Keith Terry Hinmon, and in the loving memory of my Mother, Sylvasti Hinmon.

I hope I make you and God proud.

Peace and Love to all my family and friends.

TABLE OF CONTENTS

1 Introduction

"The following historical facts are of too valuable a nature to be omitted. They throw a light upon this subject, by which any one who runs may read ; and, while they give confidence to those who are naturally timid, they strengthen the courage of those who are born to be their protectors."
-Edwin C. Holland, *A Refutation of Calumnies, 1822.*[1]

Every February, your history teachers taught you about nine historic African Americans (excluding entertainers and athletes): Martin Luther King Jr., Harriet Tubman, Malcolm X, George Washington Carver, Phyllis Wheatley, Booker T. Washington, Frederick Douglas, Rosa Parks and Thurgood Marshall. There are millions more you should know about. It is not common knowledge who decided these nine would be the only ones included in the curriculum, but it's very peculiar that four of the nine selected were former slaves and two of the nine were gunned down for trying to improve the plight of their people. Those facts aside, there are millions of Black people who you should know.

The United States government conducts a census of the population every ten years. The very first census was executed in 1790 and it revealed that there were a total of 757,181 Negroes or Black people in what was known as the United States at that time.[2] Of the 757,181 Black people in the U.S. in 1790, 697,624 were enslaved and 59,557 were free. Yes, free! In 1918, the Census Bureau published a smartly compiled 844 page analysis of Black demographics

---

[1] Edwin C. Holland, *A Refutation of The Calumnies Circulated Against The Southern & Western States, Respecting The Institution and Existence of Slavery Among Them.* Printed By A.E. Miller, Charleston, S.C. 1822. 68.
[2] In 1790, 17 states were established. The rest of the country was yet to be settled by Europeans, but was duly populated by Native Americans.

Slaves With Swag

titled *Negro Population in the United States, 1790 – 1915.* It contains invaluable information on the growth and evolution of the Black population. Here is a facsimile of one of the countless charts from the book displaying the Negro population, please look closely at the 1790 data.

Table 1	NEGRO POPULATION.							
CENSUS YEAR.		Free.		Slave.	Decennial increase.			
	Total.	Number.	Per cent.		Number.		Per cent.	
					Free.	Slave.	Free.	Slave.
1860.....	4,441,830	488,070	11.0	3,953,760	53,575	749,447	12.3	23.4
1850.....	3,638,808	434,495	11.9	3,204,313	48,202	716,958	12.5	28.8
1840.....	2,873,648	386,293	13.4	2,487,355	66,094	478,312	20.9	23.8
1830.....	2,328,642	319,599	13.7	2,009,043	85,965	471,021	36.8	30.6
1820.....	1,771,656	233,634	13.2	1,538,022	47,188	346,660	25.3	29.1
1810.....	1,377,808	186,446	13.5	1,191,362	78,011	297,760	71.9	33.3
1800.....	1,002,037	108,435	10.8	893,602	48,903	195,021	82.2	28.1
1790.....	757,181	59,557	7.9	697,624	.....	.....	.....	.....

Figure 1 In 1790, there were 757,181 Black people in the U.S. 697,624 were enslaved and 59,557 were free.[3]

During your elementary, middle and high school education, you were taught about **SOME** of the 697,624 enslaved souls. You learned how **SOME** of them got here on slave ships and how **SOME** of them were horrendously mistreated. You learned about the raggedy shacks **SOME** of them lived in and the tattered clothes **SOME** of them wore. You learned about how **SOME** of them picked cotton from sun-up to sun-down and how **SOME** of them begged their enslavers to have mercy on their poor, wretched souls. If you were educated in an American grade school, you know the story. You heard it every year from the age of 5 to 18 which unfortunately has conditioned you to assume that **ALL** Black people who lived in America prior to the ratification of the 13th Amendment in 1865 lived under those horrendous conditions. Quite frankly that couldn't be further from the truth. Yes, **SOME** did, but certainly not all.

---

[3] Department of Commerce, Bureau of the Census. *Negro Population in the United States, 1790 – 1915, 53.*

Let's fast forward for a minute to 1860. Censuses are executed every ten years, so the 1860 census was the last one performed before slavery was abolished in 1865. As of 1860, there were 4,441,830 Black people living in what was known as the United States and they made up 14.1% of the U.S. population. According to that same census, 3,953,760 of those Black souls were enslaved and almost a half million of them, 488,070 to be exact, WERE FREE!

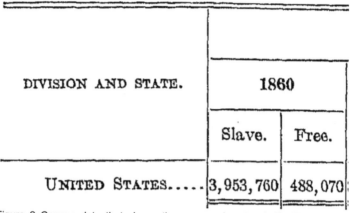

DIVISION AND STATE.	1860	
	Slave.	Free.
UNITED STATES.....	3,953,760	488,070

Figure 2 Census data that shows there were almost a half million FREE Blacks in the U.S. before the emancipation proclamation and the 13th Amendment.[4]

So, for those of you who were deceived into assuming **EVERY** Black person who lived in the U.S. prior to the ratification of the 13th Amendment to the Constitution was a slave, you now have the truth as documented by the United States Census Bureau. Almost half a million Black people roamed this country free, while other Blacks were enslaved. And they weren't just roaming it, lost and looking for a hand out. They were LIVING, WORKING, BUYING PROPERTY, RUNNING BUSINESSES, SPEAKING AND ACTING OUT AGAINST SLAVERY, RAISING FAMILIES, CREATING WEALTH, TRAVELING THE COUNTRY, SPREADING KNOWLEDGE, PREACHING THE GOSPEL, INVENTING and CREATING! Almost a half million of them! Now here's

---

[4] Department of Commerce, Bureau of the Census. *Negro Population in the United States, 1790 - 1915*, 57.

the travesty: I challenge you to name nine of them. Not nine who were escaped slaves and/or born after slavery was abolished such as Frederick Douglas, Harriet Tubman, Phyllis Wheatley. In other words, not those you learned about in school. You are challenged to name nine prominent FREE Black men and/or women who lived in the U.S. prior to 1865. Think about it...

Ok. What did you come up with? Any? Embarrassing, isn't it? You can rest assured the Census Bureau records are there, so these Brothers and Sisters existed. If you don't believe in the census, then each state kept a Register of Free Negroes that included names, birth dates and physical descriptions of these free Black folks. In addition to the register, some states even issued free Blacks certificates to prevent any misunderstandings while the free Brothers and Sisters were going about their daily business. Here is a copy of one certificate issued in 1854 to a young Black seaman named Samuel Fox:

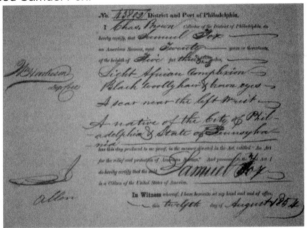

Figure 3 American Citizenship Certificate of Samuel Fox, a Black seaman from Philadelphia born about 1834.

In case you can't read the certificate, it states:

> No. 43802 District Port of Philadelphia, I Chas Brown Collector of the District of Philadelphia, do hereby certify, that Samuel Fox--- and American Seaman, aged Twenty--- years or thereabouts, of the heighth of Five feet three one/half inches,--- Slight African complexion---
> Black wooly hair + brown eyes---

A scar near the left wrist---
A native of the City of Philadelphia + State of Pennsylva-nia---
has produced to me proof, in the manner directed ia the Act,
entitled "An Act for the relief and protection of American
Seamen." And pursuant to the said Act I do hereby certify that
the said Samuel Fox--- is a Citizen of the United States of
America.--- In Witness whereof, I have hereunto set my hand
and seal of office,---this twelfth day of August 1854

So, now you know. Not every pre-1865 Black person was enslaved and Mr. Fox was just one example. In fact, pre-1865 Black people covered a wide range of social positions that can be summed up in three major categories:

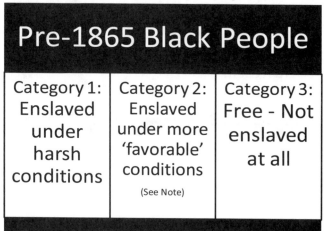

Pre-1865 Black People		
Category 1: Enslaved under harsh conditions	Category 2: Enslaved under more 'favorable' conditions (See Note)	Category 3: Free - Not enslaved at all

Figure 4 Major categorization of pre-1865 Black people. Note: The use of the word favorable is not meant to suggest any form of oppression is superior to another. Nor is it meant to downplay what the most violently oppressed Brothers and Sisters experienced. It is only used to recognize the existence of enslaved Blacks who acted against slavery and their enslavers which will be covered in much more detail later in the book.

You know all about the Category 1 Blacks and won't have an issue believing in their existence. These are the enslaved and severely oppressed Brothers and Sisters you learned about in school. You will have a hard time even believing in the existence of Category 2 and 3 Black people, which is totally understandable since you were never introduced to them during your formal education. See, if you were educated in an American public or private school, you were taught all about slaves who operated under the harshest conditions (Category

Slaves With Swag

1); probably nothing about slaves who operated under more 'favorable' conditions (Category 2); and absolutely nothing about free Blacks (Category 3).

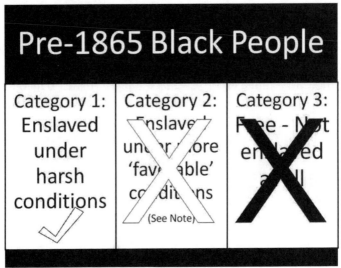

Figure 5 Graphical depiction of pre-1865 Black people.

Of the two Categories of Blacks you were not taught about (Categories 2 & 3), it will be easier for you to digest information about Category 2 Blacks, since they are more closely related to the Category 1 Blacks you know everything about. The concept of Category 3 Blacks is totally foreign to your psyche. They were Black people who were never enslaved yet lived their lives to the fullest in this country during the same time period when other Blacks were enslaved. Consequently, the Category 3 Blacks will have to be the subject of a separate book to be published at a later date. This book, *Slaves With Swag,* will focus on the Category 2 Black people: those who were slaves, but nothing like the slaves your History teachers taught you about. A solid understanding of this group will allow you to digest knowledge of Category 3 Blacks much easier.

2 Slaves

"The Negroes in our Colonies endure a slavery more compleat [sp] and attended with far worse circumstances than what any people in their condition suffer in any other part of the world, or have suffered in any other period of time."
-Edmund and William Burke as quoted in *A Caution and Warning to Great Britain and Her Colonies, in a Short Representation of the Calamitous State of the Enslaved Negroes in the British Dominions,* Anthony Benezet. 1766. [5]

Let's start with a quick review of what you learned in school. Visualize. It's anywhere between the early 1600's and late 1800's in early America. Africans are packed in the belly of ships like sardines. They are chained together and forced to urinate, defecate and vomit on themselves and each other. They are beaten and whipped only to have salt rubbed in their gaping wounds. Their tortuous journey lasts for three months and they're only allowed to come out of the belly of the ship a few minutes a week to prevent atrophy and sores. That time is also used to unchain the deceased and throw them overboard.

When those who survived the passage reach American shores, they are deemed slaves forever. They are poked, prodded, mouths greased up to give the appearance of being well fed and sold off like cattle to the highest bidder regardless of pre-existing family ties. They are broken-in on American farms and anonymously labor on the land of their oppressors from sun-up to sun-down. They slave up to 15

---

[5] Anthony Benezet, *A Caution and Warning to Great Britain and Her Colonies, In a Short Representation of the Calamitous State of the Enslaved Negroes in the British Dominions...*Philadelphia: Printed by Henry Miller in Second Street, 1766, 5.

hours a day in the summer, only to retire in the evening to a bed of hay on the dirt floor of an un-insulated, poorly constructed wood shack. They are forced to eat the pungent guts of pigs and forced to breed knowing their unborn children are predestined for the same fate. They are whipped, raped, severely oppressed, used and abused every day of their lives and their only response to all this punishment is 'yessum massuh,' 'thank you masah,' 'my massah is a good man.' They are physically, emotionally and even spiritually intimidated even though they outnumber their oppressors in some cases 15 to 1. The main method of attempting to uplift themselves is to sing in harmony or run away in the middle of the night, like a thief trying to steal their God-given freedom. They consistently pray to the good Lord to 'have mercy on their po' souls,' but are too scared to act upon the Creator's innate direction.

They have no backbone and are not willing to stand up for themselves or their fellow brethren. If one did get the guts to try and free themselves, their fellow enslaved brethren would shamelessly exhibit loyalty to their enslaver by reporting the attempt like a crab in a pot. They do not know how to read and know that their children will be just as illiterate. When out and about with their enslavers, they acknowledge their inferior position by refusing to look a White person in the eyes and they know to get off the sidewalk when walking towards any White person, even a child.

Now, if you're Black, HOW DID BEING TAUGHT THE HISTORY OF YOUR PEOPLE FROM THIS PERSPECTIVE MAKE YOU FEEL? Embarrassed? Humiliated? Disgraced? Dishonored? Shameful? Disgusted? Undignified? Degraded? Lowly? If you're not Black, how did being taught the history of Black people from this perspective make you feel about them? Do you feel sorry for them? Have a low level of respect for them because they didn't stand up for themselves? Believe they are inferior humanity? The negative imagery of Black slaves we all received in our primary education makes us all believe that every Black person in early America had no self-esteem, no sense of self worth, wore tattered clothes, and talked 'lak 'dis and 'lak 'dat. And maybe **SOME** did, but rest assured not nearly all. The exact percentages are not known, but a great many of slaves WERE PROUD PEOPLE WITH EXTREMELY HIGH SELF-ESTEEM, SPOKE GOOD ENGLISH, WORE NICE CLOTHES (you will have examples in a minute), WORKED HARD FOR THEIR FAMLIES, AND TRAVELED AS THEY PLEASED! THEY FOUGHT, WERE EDUCATED, AND POSSESSED FREEDOM AS WELL AS MONEY!

Now, due to what you were taught and the blind promotion of those negative concepts, you are probably under the false impression that every Black slave in the United States was just the humblest, most ragged, poor, and wretched shell of a human you ever saw. But take a minute and think about the schematics and apply some good old fashioned common sense to the situation. Whenever the topic of slavery is discussed and you inevitably think about what you would do in that situation, don't you always say 'I couldn't have been nobody's slave. I would've done A, B, C, D AND E!' Now, don't you think somebody back then actually said that? Where in the world do you think you got that fighting spirit from?

Don't Black people today cover a wide gamut of abilities, thoughts and actions? Now, don't you think those Black people back then would cover a wide spectrum as well? Think about it. Black people today have a wide variety in abilities, thoughts and actions. They cover a very wide spectrum of characteristics: educated to ignorant; intelligent to simpleton; jovial to depressed; mature to immature; alcoholic to sober; addicted to uncontaminated.[6] Guess

---

[6] In actuality all cultures within the human race have people who exhibit these same characteristics. They are characteristics of the human race.

what? Black people back then covered that same spectrum, even the enslaved ones. So, while you may be under the very FALSE impression that a) All pre-1865 Negroes were enslaved, you may even be under the more grossly false impression that b) all those slaves were ignorant, passive, 'yes massah, gwine git dat der' type slaves, which couldn't be further from the truth. You don't have to be a PhD to figure that out. You already had that feeling deep down in your gut that told you so. The only thing you're missing is the tangible proof to validate that gut feeling which, lucky for you, is contained in the following pages of this book.

This book represents omitted, left out, deleted, or whatever you want to call it, chapters of Black History. And although it is LOADED with knowledge, it only skims the surface of the depths of Black people. Its purpose is to destroy the idea of Black inferiority in global society's general thought. The magnitude of this task is daunting given the manner in which the Black inferiority concept was relentlessly driven in the brains of every American taught under the standardized curriculum, but this text is up for the challenge. It is heavily armed with WELL-DOCUMENTED HISTORIES of Africans in America in the 1700's and 1800's, including their accomplishments, triumphs, and most importantly their pictures. The knowledge of these Brothers and Sisters existence and the magnitude of their accomplishments will finitely counteract all the negative aspects of Black American history (including the negative imagery) you received in grades K-12.

This book is the medicine required to repair your cultural self-esteem from the damage it received by learning Blacks were docile creatures who allowed themselves to be enslaved and were too ignorant, stupid and lazy to do anything except mindlessly labor in the fields for their enslavers. This book has the grand task of convincing you that early American Blacks were more than just ugly, nappy-headed, 'gwine do dis massah' and 'gwine do dat massah' type folk who were inferior to White people in every way shape and form. These concepts were burned into your brain during your early years and reinforced in your adult years via movies, music, news, etc., so we have a lot of ground to cover. You will learn first-hand account examples to include names, dates, places and pictures that will change your perception of early American Black people forever! So without further ado, let's begin.

A brief dramatic pause is required here to emphasize the magnitude of the knowledge you are about to absorb. You are about to experience the kind of self-knowledge that will satisfy your mind, body and soul and undoubtedly boost your cultural self-esteem. Please be excited about the opportunity. It is imperative that you take a few seconds to find a spot way in the back of your brain to place your current ideology of ALL slaves which is probably very similar to the description provided at the beginning of this chapter. Make room for the rest of the story because here it comes...

3 Fighting Slaves

"He that stealeth a man, and selleth him, or if he be found in his hand, he shall surely be put to death."
-Exodus, 21:16

Slaves fought. Let's say it again, SLAVES FOUGHT! They all didn't just stand around and watch while their fellow brothers and sisters were whipped. They fought. They didn't all just go willingly to the whipping post to have their blood spilled on the ground by some overseer, they fought. Little Isaac Burgan fought. Isaac Burgan was born a slave in 1848 in Marion, North Carolina. His life story was profiled in a book titled *Men of Mark: Eminent, Progressive and Rising* written by Dr. William J. Simmons in 1887. This William J. Simmons is not the William J. Simmons who resurrected the Ku Klux Klan. This William J. Simmons was Black and born a slave in Charleston, South Carolina in 1849. After escaping from slavery, Dr. Simmons heavily pursued an education and earned a Bachelor degree from Howard University in 1873 and a Masters also from Howard in 1881. Dr. Simmons was a trained educator and worked his way up to become the Principal of Hillsdale Public School in the District of Columbia. He ultimately ended up as the President of State University of Kentucky which was originally known as the Kentucky Baptist Normal and Theological Institute and ultimately renamed Simmons College of Kentucky after this great man.[7] In his spare time Dr. Simmons wrote the 1,138 page *Men of Mark*.

---

[7] Simmons College of Kentucky is still in operation. Visit www.simmonscollegeky.edu.

Slaves With Swag

In the book, Dr. Simmons describes one of Mr. Isaac Burgan's run-ins with an overseer while he was still a young slave as follows:

> The sorest conflict of his recollection grew out of an attempt on the part of the authorities to whip his mother. When the cruel work began young Burgan hastened to the scene. Here with bare feet and tattered garments he stood merely looking on till the screams of a loving mother pierced his heart to its depths. Then seizing a large poker he struck the man a telling blow on the back of the head. The brutal arm dropped and the lash was staid. Isaac fled for his life but soon returned, and in a few days got a double portion of that from which he saved his mother.[8]

Imagine that! A young slave boy standing there listening to the wails of his mother as her flesh was split open by the hastened tail of a bloody whip! Picture young Isaac grabbing a poker and whacking the back of the head of the unexpected assailant! Now, did young Isaac get it in the end? Yes. But you can rest assured he was well aware of the consequences before he struck, yet was willing to make that sacrifice for the preservation of his mother. Here are pictures of Dr. Simmons who recorded the story and Mr. Burgan, both as adults.

Figure 6 Rev. William J. Simmons (left) and Isaac M. Burgan.

If you're having trouble believing these facts, please go to your web browser and/or local library and look them up.

---

[8] William J. Simmons. *Men of Mark: Eminent, Progressive and Rising.* Cleveland: Geo. M. Rewell & Co., 1887. 1,087.

This is just one example of many that you will read about in this text, so if you need to pull the provided reference and some references of your own to convince yourself, then please do so now. You must open your mind's eye to accept this knowledge as it will be unlike anything you learned in school. You were not taught this history in school and at this point it doesn't matter why because you are literally holding the power of knowledge in your hand. Dr. Simmons chose to highlight Mr. Burgan's life for reasons other than the defense of his mother and the rest of Mr. Burgan's accomplishments will be covered later in the text. For now, let's examine other slaves who fought as Mr. Burgan was hardly alone.

It is common knowledge that slaves ran away from bondage, but it is assumed they all ran away barefoot, shirtless, cold, hungry and cowering in the middle of the night. And SOME may have, but assuredly not all. Barnaby Grigby, his wife Mary Elizabeth, his compatriots Frank Wanzer, Emily Foster a.k.a. Ann Wood and two other unnamed slaves certainly didn't leave that way. This proud group left their enslaver's plantations in Loudon County, Virginia on December 24th, 1855 and they gave themselves a few Christmas gifts on the way out. This group didn't leave barefoot, shirtless, cold, hungry and cowering in the middle of the night. In fact, they didn't even leave on foot. When this group set out for freedom, some were on horseback and others were in a carriage. Who's carriage? Why, one of their former enslaver's carriage being pulled by his best horses. And guess what else they took when they departed Loudon County, Virginia? They took some of the man's good knives and pistols. Yes, pistols! When they reached Hoods Mill, Maryland they were approached by six White men and a boy who questioned who they were, where they were headed and if they had any credentials to prove it? Here is what followed:

> At this juncture, the fugitives verily believing that the time had arrived for the practical use of their pistols and dirks, pulled them out of their concealment—the young women as well as

the young men—and declared they would not be "taken!" One of the white men raised his gun, pointing the muzzle directly towards one of the young women, with the threat that he would "shoot," etc. "Shoot! shoot!! shoot!!!" she exclaimed, with a double barrelled pistol in one hand and a long dirk knife in the other, utterly unterrified and fully ready for a death struggle. The male leader of the fugitives by this time had "pulled back the hammers" of his "pistols," and was about to fire! Their adversaries seeing the weapons, and the unflinching determination on the part of the *runaways* to stand their ground, "spill blood, kill, or die," rather than be "taken," very prudently "sidled over to the other side of the road," leaving at least four of the victors to travel on their way.[9]

Slaves fought. This history of Barnaby Grigby and his noble compatriots was documented in a book titled *The Underground Railroad* originally published in 1872 by a man named William Still. William Still was a Black man, a FREE Black man, meaning he had never been a slave. His house in Philadelphia was a stop on the Underground Railroad.

Figure 7 Portrait of William Still. He resided at 244 S. 12th Street in Philadelphia. The Historical Society erected a marker at his old residence. If you live in or visit Philadelphia, stop by and feel the power of his presence.

Since Mr. Still was Black, free, educated and wealthy he had the resources to not only provide for the escaped slaves as they passed through the City of Brotherly Love, but to also document each of their stories. His original intent of writing those stories down was to help other escaped slaves locate

---

[9] William Still. *Underground Railroad Records rev. ed.* Philadelphia: William Still Publisher, 1886. 125. All quotations from the 1886 revised edition.

their family members, but after slavery was over Mr. Still had the foresight to formally publish them in *The Underground Railroad*. In addition to assisting escaped slaves and authoring an important book, Mr. Still owned a successful coal business and a very large meeting hall.[10] Consequently, he could afford to have images drawn and inserted in the book. So, here is the image of Barnaby Grigby, his wife Mary Elizabeth, Frank Wanzer, Emily Foster a.k.a. Ann Wood, one of the two other unnamed slaves, the stolen carriage, horses, and pistols from *The Underground Railroad* written and published in the late 1800's by William Still, a free Black man.

Figure 8 Barnaby Grigby and his compatriots taking a stand![11]

Mr. Grigby's party wasn't the only one who started out for freedom fully armed. Misters Jim Scott, Tom Pennington, Sam Scott, Bill Scott, Abe Bacon and Jack Wells who were slaves of the Honorable L. McLane (Secretary to President Jackson[12]) also started for freedom with the appropriate hardware. Their story was also documented in

---

[10] Simmons,149-61.
[11] Still, unnumbered page before page 125.
[12] John C.Rives. *The Congressional Globe for the Second Session, Thirty-Second Congress*...New Series Vol. XXVII. Washington D.C. 1853. 255.

Slaves With Swag

Mr. Still's *The Underground Railroad*. As they headed from Cecil County, Maryland, Mr. Still noted:

> ...they were strongly armed. Sam had a large horse pistol and a butcher knife ; Jack had a revolver ; Abe had a double-barrelled pistol and a large knife ; Jim had a single-barrelled pistol and counted on 'blowing a man down if any one touched' him. Bill also had a single-barrelled pistol, and when he started resolved to 'come through or die.'[13]

Yes, slaves fought. Wesley Harris and the Matterson brothers, they fought. Mr. Still describes Mr. Harris as being "twenty-two years ; dark color ; medium height ; and of slender stature."[14] Wesley decided to "go off" because "About a month before Wesley left, the overseer, for some trifling cause, attempted to flog him, but was resisted, and himself flogged."[15] Slaves fought. Partially through their trip, Wesley and his companions spent the night in the barn of a White man where the following took place:

> About noon men were heard talking around the barn. I woke my companions up and told them that that man had betrayed us. At first they did not believe me. In a moment afterwards the barn door was opened, and in came the men, eight in number. One of the men asked the owner of the barn if he had any long straw. 'Yes,' was the answer. So up on the mow came three of the men, when, to their great surprise, as they pretended, we were discovered. The question was then asked the owner of the barn by one of the men, if he harbored runaway negroes in his barn? He answered, 'No,' and pretended to be entirely ignorant of their being in his barn. One of the men replied that four negroes were on the mow, and he knew of it. The men then asked us where we were going. We told them to Gettysburg, that we had aunts and a mother there. Also we spoke of a Mr. Houghman, a gentleman we happened to have some knowledge of, having seen him in Virginia. We were next asked for our passes. We told them that we hadn't any, that we had not been required to carry them where we came from. They then said that we would have to go before a magistrate, and if he allowed us to go on, well and good. The men all being armed and furnished with ropes, we were ordered to be tied. I told them if they took me they would have to take me dead or crippled. At that instant one of my friends cried out—'Where is the man that betrayed us?' Spying him at the same moment, he shot him (badly wounding him). Then the conflict fairly began.

---

[13] Still, 433.
[14] Still, 48.
[15] Still, 49.

The constable seized me by the collar, or rather behind my shoulder. I at once shot him with my pistol, but in consequence of his throwing up his arm, which hit mine as I fired, the effect of the load of my pistol was much turned aside; his face, however, was badly burned, besides his shoulder being wounded. I again fired on the pursuers, but do not know whether I hit anybody or not. I then drew a sword, I had brought with me, and was about cutting my way to the door, when I was shot by one of the men, receiving the entire contents of one load of a double barreled gun in my left arm, that being the arm with which I was defending myself. The load brought me to the ground, and I was unable to make further struggle for myself. I was then badly beaten with guns, &c. In the meantime, my friend Craven, who was defending himself, was shot badly in the face, and most violently beaten until he was conquered and tied.[16]

Mr. Still thought Wesley Harris and the Matterson Brothers' epic battle for their freedom was also worth documenting with a drawing. Here it is:

Figure 9 Wesley Harris and the Matterson brothers, slaves who fought. Notice Wesley's pistol smoke next to the left ear of his assailant.[17]

If you're paying attention as you're reading, then you're probably wondering if Wesley was captured, how did he ever make it to Philadelphia to tell his story to Mr. Still? Well, the rest of Wesley's story is as follows:

---

[16] Still, 50.
[17] Still, unnumbered page before page 51.

Slaves With Swag

...I was made a prisoner at a tavern, kept by a man named Fisher. There my wounds were dressed, and thirty-two shot were taken from my arm. For three days, I was crazy, and they thought I would die. During the first two weeks, while I was a prisoner at the tavern, I raised a great deal of blood, and was considered in a very dangerous condition-so much so that persons desiring to see me were not permitted. Afterwards I began to get better, and was then kept very privately-was strictly watched day and night. Occasionally, however, the cook, a colored woman (Mrs. Smith), would manage to see me. Also James Matthews succeeded in getting to see me; consequently, as my wounds healed and my senses came to me, I began to plan how to make another effort to escape. I asked one of the friends, alluded to above, to get me a rope. He got it. I kept it about me four days in my pocket; in the meantime I procured three nails. On Friday night, October 14th, I fastened my nails in under the window sill ; tied my rope to the nails, threw my shoes out of the window, put the rope in my mouth, then took hold of it with my well hand, clambered into the window, very weak, but I managed to let myself down to the ground. I was so weak, that I could scarcely walk, but I managed to hobble off to a place three quarters of a mile from the tavern, where a friend had fixed upon for me to go, if I succeeded in making my escape. There I was found by my friend, who kept me secure till Saturday eve, when a swift horse was furnished by James Rogers, and a colored man found to conduct me to Gettysburg. Instead of going direct to Gettysburg, we took a different road, in order to shun our pursuers, as the news of my escape had created general excitement.[18]

Unfortunately, his companions, the Matterson Brothers, were sold back into slavery. They were fighters through and through.

The July 12, 1785 Charleston Evening Gazette reported the following incident:

We learn from Providence that a negro belonging to Mr. Barron, having eloped, such a pursuit was made after him that he thought it proper to return. It is the practice of runaway slaves in Providence, to besmear themselves with grease, so that it is almost impossible for their pursuers to hold them; thus besmeared, and armed with a large knife, Mr. Barron received information of the slave being in the negroe quarters; as it was determined that he should be punished, his master, Mr. Car and Mr. McKinnon went into the quarters to secure him. Two of the company went into the quarters, whilst Mr. Car guarded the door; the fellow being thus at bay, made a desperate effort to get away, but being seized by Mr. Car, he drew a concealed knife, and stabbed the unhappy gentleman to the heart so that he instantly died. Mr. McKinnon pursued him, and would have

---

[18] Still, 50-1.

26

secured him but for the greasy condition of his skin ; in struggling with him he received several gashes, some of them so well directed that if the knife had not been previously blunted in stabbing the other gentleman, he must inevitably have fallen...[19]

And here is a copy of the actual article from the actual paper. When reading these old articles, you will notice the lower case 's' is somewhat elongated making it look a lot like a lower case 'f'. Please note the difference:

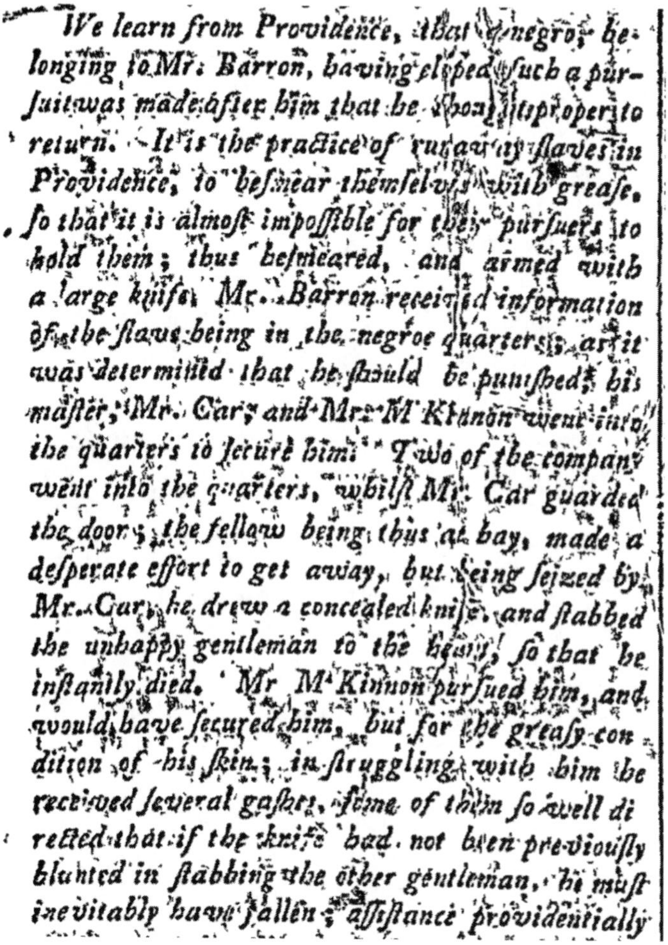

Figure 10 American newspaper article documenting the actions of a fighting slave.

[19] Charleston Evening Gazette, July 12, 1785. 2.

Slaves With Swag

The September 2, 1826 issue of the Niles Weekly Register contained the following excerpt:

> The following case happened last Monday: a white man had undertaken to inflict personal punishment on a black woman, not his slave, but she was not content to bear it long, and turned upon him and chastised him for beating her. For this she was brought before a magistrate, under an old law which authorizes cropping for the offence in a black, of defending him or herself, in returning the assault and battery of a white person. But the case was dismissed.[20]

Please believe the term 'turned upon him' used in the article means 'she put hands on him'. It kind of gives you a picture of Della Reese's character in the movie Harlem Nights, except this lady walked away with her pinky toe still in tact. I guess he ran up on the wrong one that day! And to top it all off, the magistrate dismissed the case! Assuredly, both his and her associates had to get a chuckle out of the whole ordeal.

Not so amusing is the account from the March 15, 1856 Columbus Tri-Weekly Enquirer that describes the following altercation that occurred on the John B. Lampkin plantation in Hancock County, Mississippi:

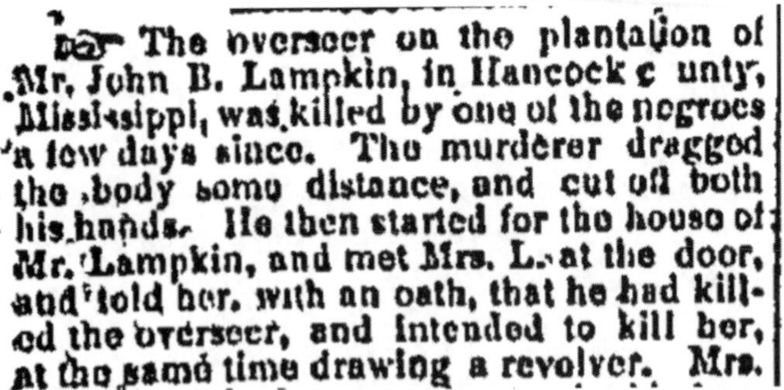

☞ The overseer on the plantation of
Mr. John B. Lampkin, in Hancock c unty,
Mississippi, was killed by one of the negroes
a few days since. The murderer dragged
the body some distance, and cut off both
his hands. He then started for the house of
Mr. Lampkin, and met Mrs. L. at the door,
and told her, with an oath, that he had killed the overseer, and intended to kill her,
at the same time drawing a revolver. Mrs.

Figure 11 American newspaper article documenting the actions of a fighting slave.[21]

The overseer mentioned in the article certainly wasn't the only to be eradicated by those he abused. The December 17, 1842 New York Spectator informed the public of another

---

[20] H. Niles & Son, ed. *Niles Weekly Register, Documents, Essays and Facts Together with Notices of the Arts and Manufacture, and a Record of the Events of the Times From September 1826, to March 1827- Vol. XXXI or, Volume VII-Third Series.* Baltimore: Franklin Press, 1827. 25.
[21] Columbus Tri-Weekly Enquirer, Mar. 15, 1856. 2.

overseer who met a similar fate down in Terrebonne, Louisiana:

> ☞ A few days ago, in the parish of Terrebonne, Louisiana, a slave named William, belonging to the plantation of Mrs. Fields, killed the overseer, Mr. S. H. Somers, by a blow with a wooden lever on the back of the neck. The slave, having been slightly corrected by the overseer, murdered him in revenge. He then sought the sheriff, confessed his crime, and said that he wished to be punished immediately. He was not sorry for what he had done, but stated that he had made up his mind to the deed some time before.

Figure 12 American newspaper article documenting the actions of a fighting slave.[22]

The end result of yet another overseer murder that occurred in Matagorda County, Texas was reported in the October 29, 1847 Daily Picayune:

> ☞ A negro who killed the overseer of the plantation of Mr. R. S. Blount, in Matagorda county, Texas, has been hung.

Figure 13 American newspaper article documenting the actions of a fighting slave.[23]

According to *A Documentary History of American Industrial Society*, the December 7, 1774 Georgia Gazette gave the following account of slaves who fought:

> From St. Andrew's Parish we have the following melancholy account, viz. That on Tuesday morning the 29th ult. six new Negro fellows and four wenches, belonging to Capt. Morris, killed the Overseer in the field, after which they went to the house, murdered his wife, and dangerously wounded a carpenter named Wright, also a boy who died next day; they then proceeded to the house of Angus McIntosh, whom they likewise dangerously wounded ; and being there joined by a sensible fellow, the property of said McIntosh, they went to the house of Roderick M'Leod, wounded him very much, and killed his son, who had fired upon them on their coming up and broke the arm of the fellow who had joined them. Their leader and McIntosh's negro have been taken and burnt, and two of the wenches have returned to the plantation.[24]

---

[22] New York Spectator, Dec. 17, 1842. 3.
[23] Daily Picayune, Oct. 29, 1847. 2.
[24] John R. Commons, et. al. ed. *A Documentary History of American Industrial Society vol. II.* Cleveland: Arthur H. Clark Co., 1910. 118-9.

Slaves With Swag

The record of slave trials for Baldwin County, Georgia between 1812 and 1832 were documented in *The American Historical Association's Annual Report of 1903*. The records give quite a few accounts of slaves who fought. On February 17, 1819 a slave named Rodney, whose enslaver was Maj. John A. Jones, was charged with arson; on January 19, 1822 a slave named Davis, whose enslaver was William Johns, was charged with "assault with intent to kill a white person;" On December 5, 1825 the records show that a slave named Stephen, whose enslaver was Israel T. Jordan, was charged with "assault with intent to kill a free white man;" and on July 8, 1829 a slave named Caroline whose enslaver was Robert B. Washington was charged with "maiming a free white person."[25] Slaves fought!

James Lewis was born a slave in Woodville, Wilkinson County, Mississippi in 1832 and he fought. When the Civil War broke out, James was a slave steward on the Confederate Ship *De Soto*. While near Columbus Island, James heard the rumor that President Lincoln was planning to sign the Emancipation Proclamation and that news alone was enough to convince him to make a stand. He heard the Union Army had recently taken New Orleans, so that's where he headed. Once he reached New Orleans, he joined the Union Army then gained approval to start a Colored Regiment of troops. Before he was done Col. James Lewis established two companies of colored infantry. Here is the esteemed Colonel James Lewis:

---

[25] American Historical Society. Annual Report of the American Historical Association for the Year 1903 vol. II. Washington, D.C.: Government printing Office, 1904. 461-6. Their verdicts varied from hanging to not guilty.

Figure 14 Colonel James Lewis who was born a slave in Wilkinson County, Mississippi.

After the war the good Colonel was appointed to the following posts:

- Traveling Agent of the Freedmen's Bureau educational department where he established new schools for ex-slaves
- Inspector of Customs in Louisiana by the Honorable William P. Kellogg
- Captain of the Metropolitan police
- Colonel of the Second Regiment State Militia by Governor Warmouth
- Naval Officer of the Port at New Orleans by President Hayes
- Superintendent of the United States bonded warehouse in New Orleans by Judge Folger who was Secretary of the Treasury

The Louisiana Standard published the following article about Colonel Lewis on January 19, 1884:

> We note with pleasure the confirmation of Colonel James Lewis as surveyor-general of Louisiana, by the Senate last Tuesday. Colonel Lewis has, during the course of a busy, active, political life, filled many important State and Federal positions, notably those of administrator of police and administrator of improvements of this great city, and naval officer at this port, with credit and honor to himself, his party and his race. His confirmation by the Senate is but a just recognition of his

services as a Republican and his worth as a citizen, and is
heartily approved by the masses of the people.[26]

But before his later accomplishments, James Lewis was a
slave who fought.[27]

The previous entries are all examples of individual or
very small groups of slaves who fought. However, there are
countless incidences of much larger groups of slaves banding
together to usurp power from their oppressors. These battles
are formally called slave revolts or slave insurrections. Three
of these revolts have been relatively popularized: one
organized in 1800 by General Gabriel in Richmond; another
in 1822 by Denmark Vesey in Charleston, South Carolina;
and another in 1831 lead by Nat Turner in South Hampton,
Virginia. But these three only represent three out of hundreds
of revolts lead by slaves. And oddly enough, two of these
three popularized (the first two) were quelled by fellow slaves
who alerted authorities of the plans. The third revolt however,
was executed in grand fashion by Nat Turner who was born a
slave in South Hampton, Virginia in 1800. In *The Confessions
of Nat Turner* the warrior stated:

> ...I had a vision - and I saw white spirits and black spirits
> engaged in battle, and the sun was darkened - the thunder
> rolled in the Heavens, and blood flowed in streams - and I
> heard a voice saying, 'Such is your luck, such you are called to
> see, and let it come rough or smooth, you must surely bear it.[28]

Out of that dream, Nat formulated a plan and struck a blow
for the enslaved. He and his compatriots killed 55 of their
oppressors in their struggle for freedom.

On September 9, 1739, a group of slaves near the
Stono River in St. Paul's Parish in South Carolina (which was
not far from Charleston) banded together to revolt. At that
time, the Carolinas was a colony of England and the then

---

[26] Simmons, 958.
[27] Simmons, 954-958.
[28] Thomas R. Gray, *The Confessions of Nat Turner, The Leader of the Late
Insurrection in Southampton, VA. As Fully and Voluntarily Made to Thomas
R. Gray...* Richmond: Thomas R. Gray, 1832. 8.

Lieutenant Governor of the Province, William Bull, wrote a letter to England describing the revolt.[29] Mr. Bull stated:

> My Lords, I beg leave to lay before your Lordships an account of our Affairs, first in regard to the Desertion of our Negroes. . . On the 9th of September last at Night a great Number of Negroes Arose in Rebellion, broke open a Store where they got arms, killed twenty one White Persons, and were marching the next morning in a Daring manner out of the Province, killing all they met and burning several Houses as they passed along the Road.[30]

A man named Alexander Hewatt described the procession of these same Freedom Fighters in his 1779 book titled An Historical Account of the Rise and Progress of the Colonies of South Carolina and Georgia as follows:

> While Carolina was kept in a state of constant fear and agitation from this quarter, an insurrection openly broke out in the heart of the settlement which alarmed the whole province. A number of negroes having assembled together at Stono, first surprised and killed two young men in a ware-house, and then plundered it of guns and ammunition. Being thus provided with arms, they elected one of their number captain, and agreed to follow him, marching towards the south-west, with colours flying and drums beating, like a disciplined company. They forcibly entered the house of Mr. Godfrey, and having murdered him, his wife, and children, they took all the arms he had in it, set fire to the house, and then proceeded towards Jacksonsburgh. In their way they plundered and burnt every house...killing every white person they found in them, and compelling the Negroes to join them.[31]

This was not the only rebellion in South Carolina in 1739. In his book titled An Account of Some of the Principal Slave Insurrections, Joshua Coffin states "In 1739, there were three formidable insurrections of the slaves in South Carolina.-one in St. Paul's Parish, one in St. Johns, and one in Charleston."[32]

---

[29] Joseph Cephas Carroll. Slave Insurrections in the United States,1800-1865. (Boston: Chapman & Grimes, 1938 : Mineola, NY: Dover Publications Inc, 2004). 24.
[30] Lieutenant Governor William Bull letter to Duke of New Castle documenting slave insurrection.
http://www.pbs.org/wgbh/aia/part1/1h311t.html
[31] Alexander Hewatt. An Historical Account of the Rise and Progress of the Colonies of South Carolina and Georgia, vol. II. London, 1779. 72.
[32] Joshua Coffin. An Account of Some of the Principal Slave Insurrections... New York: American Anti-slavery Society, 1860. 14.

Slaves With Swag

The citizens of Midgeville, Georgia got a hearty warning of insurrections in the December 23, 1856 *Federal Union* newspaper. The paper exclaimed:

> We have refrained from giving our readers any of the accounts of contemplated negro insurrections that have been lately discovered in the South Western States, and even in Virginia and South Carolina. It is a delicate subject to touch, but it would be criminal to keep the public in ignorance of matters so vitally important. It is the right of every man to know when such a danger is at hand, and it is his duty to provide effectually against it. Better be a little too cautious than to suffer from overweening confidence.[33]

And it seems their warning was valid as the following incident was reported on page 3 of the May 26, 1857 Federal Union:

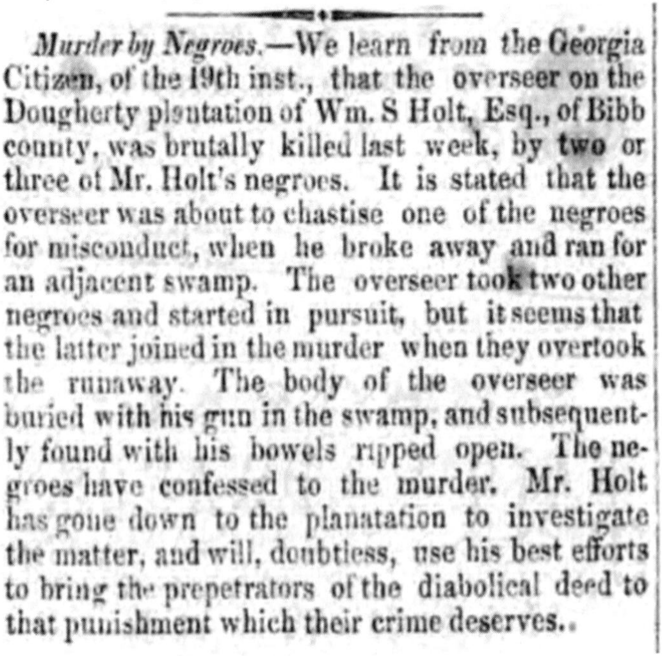

Murder by Negroes.—We learn from the Georgia Citizen, of the 19th inst., that the overseer on the Dougherty plantation of Wm. S Holt, Esq., of Bibb county, was brutally killed last week, by two or three of Mr. Holt's negroes. It is stated that the overseer was about to chastise one of the negroes for misconduct, when he broke away and ran for an adjacent swamp. The overseer took two other negroes and started in pursuit, but it seems that the latter joined in the murder when they overtook the runaway. The body of the overseer was buried with his gun in the swamp, and subsequently found with his bowels ripped open. The negroes have confessed to the murder. Mr. Holt has gone down to the planatation to investigate the matter, and will, doubtless, use his best efforts to bring the prepetrators of the diabolical deed to that punishment which their crime deserves.

Figure 15 American newspaper article documenting the actions of fighting slaves.[34]

Georgia residents were also aware of the following specific incident involving fighting slaves as reported in the December 21, 1799 Charleston City Gazette:

---

[33] A *Documentary History of American Industrial Society vol. II*, 116.
[34] A Documentary History of American Industrial Society vol. II, 119.

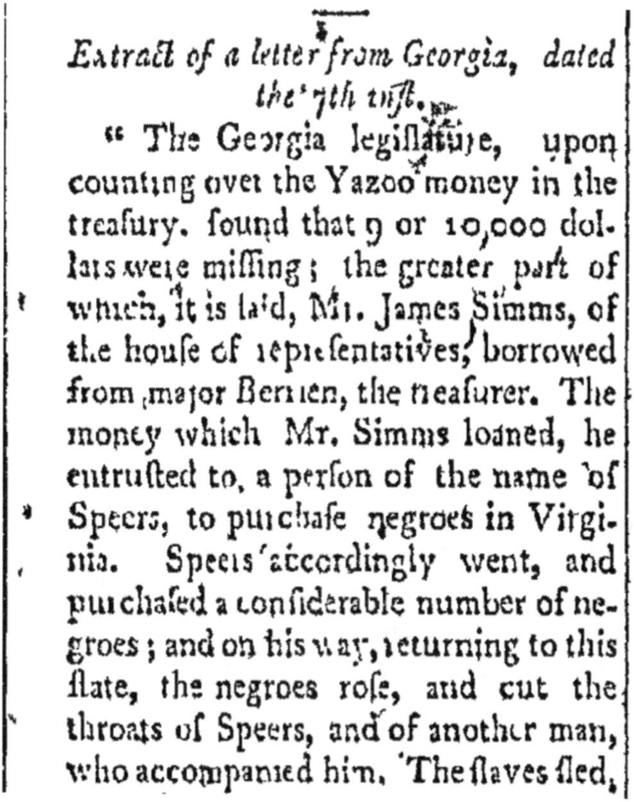

Extract of a letter from Georgia, dated the 7th inst.

" The Georgia legiflature, upon counting over the Yazoo money in the treafury. found that 9 or 10,000 dollars were miffing ; the greater part of which, it is la'd, Mr. James Simms, of the houfe of reprefentatives, borrowed from major Berrien, the treafurer. The money which Mr. Simms loaned, he entrufted to, a perfon of the name of Speers, to purchafe negroes in Virginia. Speers accordingly went, and purchafed a confiderable number of negroes ; and on his way, returning to this flate, the negroes rofe, and cut the throats of Speers, and of another man, who accompanied him, The flaves fled.

Figure 16 American newspaper documenting the actions of fighting slaves.[35]

It seems Mr. Simms planned to 'flip' the slaves with "borrowed" i.e. stolen money, but he didn't plan on those slaves fighting back. That miscalculation cost Mr. Simms his reputation and political career, and unfortunately cost Mr. Speers his life.

In Delaware in 1861, a group of enslavers noticed their slaves having quite a few funerals for their deceased brethren. After the various enslavers began talking, none could account for the dead slaves, which piqued their curiosity. The Whites decided to dig up the bodies of the dead to see exactly who's dead slaves were buried in there.

---

[35] Charleston City Gazette, *Extract from a news letter from Georgia, dated Dec. 7*, Dec. 21, 1799. 3.

Slaves With Swag

Joseph Cephas Carroll described in his book *Slave Insurrections in the United States, 1800-1865* that, "They found the coffins all right, but instead of being filled with dead Negroes, they were filled to the brim with muskets and ammunition."[36]

Slaves fought people. Many of them fought while still on the slave ship before they even landed on American soil. There have been countless slave revolts on board the cursed vessels. One ship revolt you may have heard was led by a native African named Cinque. The revolt took place on board the schooner Amistad. You may know about this revolt because the movie *Amistad* released in 1997 was based on it. The real Amistad revolt took place late June/early July 1839. The Amistad ship, captained by a man named Ramon Ferrer, left from Havana, Cuba and was heading for Principe, Cuba, but it never made it there. The Amistad had 53 Negroes on-board and Cinque organized the men for battle. They killed Captain Ferrer and the cook but let the rest of the crew go with the exception of the ship's owner Jose Ruiz and crew member Pedro Montes who had some nautical knowledge. If you saw the movie you know the rest of the story. Cinque demanded Ruiz take them back to Africa, and Ruiz headed in that direction during the day as the Africans could tell their general direction based on the sun's position. But at night, Ruiz would steer the ship back West since it was more difficult for the African's to read his deceit. The ship went about this back and forth motion until August 26, 1839 when it was taken by the U.S. Navy near the Long Island Sound. After a two year trial, with the help of John Quincy Adams, the Africans were released and sent back to Africa with the help of the American Missionary Association.[37] Here is a picture documenting the initial takeover on the schooner

[36] Carroll, 204.
[37] Coffin, 33-4. Carroll, 179-80. Barber, John W. *A History of the Amistad Captives*, New Haven: E.L. & J.W. Barber, 1840.

Amistad from John Barber's *A History of the Amistad Captives:*

Death of Capt. Ferrer, the Captain of the Amistad, July, 1839.

Figure 17 Documentation of the slave revolt on board the Amistad which was lead by the African Cinque.

Captain George Scott's load of slaves revolted against him and his crew on their way from Guinea to the Atlantic coast. The May 3, 1731 issue of the Boston Gazette included an account of the incident as written by Captain Scott himself:

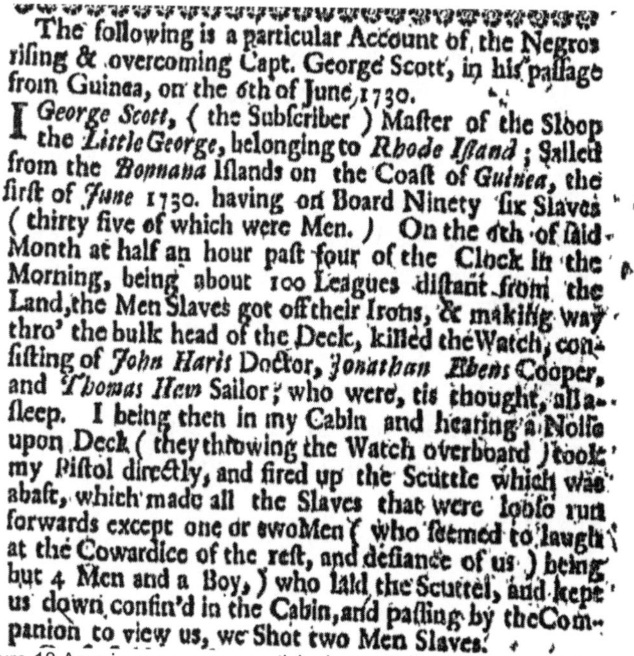

The following is a particular Account of the Negros rifing & overcoming Capt. George Scott, in his paſſage from Guinea, on the 6th of June, 1730.

I George Scott, (the Subſcriber) Maſter of the Sloop the *Little George*, belonging to *Rhode Iſland* ; Sailed from the *Bonnana* Iſlands on the Coaſt of *Guinea*, the firſt of *June* 1730. having on Board Ninety ſix Slaves (thirty five of which were Men.) On the 6th of ſaid Month at half an hour paſt four of the Clock in the Morning, being about 100 Leagues diſtant from the Land, the Men Slaves got off their Irons, & making way thro' the bulk head of the Deck, killed the Watch, conſiſting of *John Harit* Doctor, *Jonathan Ebens* Cooper, and *Thomas Ham* Sailor; who were, tis thought, all aſleep. I being then in my Cabin and hearing a Noiſe upon Deck (they throwing the Watch overboard) took my Piſtol directly, and fired up the Scuttle which was abaft, which made all the Slaves that were loſſo run forwards except one or twoMen (who ſeemed to laugh at the Cowardice of the reſt, and defiance of us) being but 4 Men and a Boy,) who laid the Scuttel, and kept us down confin'd in the Cabin, and paſſing by the Companion to view us, we Shot two Men Slaves.

Figure 18 American newspaper article documenting the actions of fighting slaves.[38]

---

[38] Boston Gazette, May 3, 1731. 1.

Slaves With Swag

At the end of the affair, Captain Scott's whole crew perished during the battle with the exception of himself and a cabin boy.[39]

Joshua Coffin in *An Account of Some of the Principle Slave Insurrections* mentioned a slave revolt that took place on Captain John Major's ship in 1732. He notes that the whole crew was murdered, including the Captain, and all goods on board the ship were seized by the Negroes.[40] Another revolt took place on the ship Dolphin of London on the coast of Africa. The September 29, 1735 Boston Post Boy paper gave an account of the event as follows:

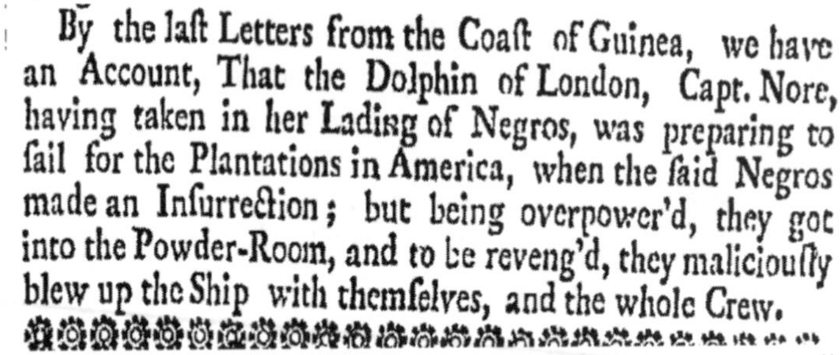

> By the laſt Letters from the Coaſt of Guinea, we have an Account, That the Dolphin of London, Capt. Nore, having taken in her Lading of Negros, was preparing to ſail for the Plantations in America, when the ſaid Negros made an Inſurrection; but being overpower'd, they got into the Powder-Room, and to be reveng'd, they maliciouſly blew up the Ship with themſelves, and the whole Crew.

Figure 19 American newspaper documenting the actions of fighting slaves.[41]

Yet another revolt was executed by slaves on a Rhode Island slave ship in 1747. The Captain of the ship, Captain Beers, and most of his crew, except two, perished in that battle.[42]

Another successful revolt was executed by the slaves on board the brig Creole which left Richmond, Virginia October 27, 1841 headed to New Orleans. The battle was captured in the December 3, 1841 issue of *The Daily Picayune*.[43] Here is a facsimile of that article:

---

[39] Coffin, 14.
[40] Coffin, 14. Carroll 20.
[41] Boston Post Boy, Sep. 29, 1735.3.
[42] Coffin, 15. Carroll, 31.
[43] Coffin 34. Carroll 181.

Mutiny and Murder.

Our community was thrown into considerable excitement yesterday, by the arrival of the brig Creole, with the intelligence that 135 slaves on board had risen, in the vicinity of the island of Abaco, murdered a passenger, severely wounded the Captain, and forced the vessel into Nassau, New Providence, where most of the slaves were set at liberty by the British authorities. We have the particulars of this outrage from Mr. Goddard, the former mate, and now the master of the Creole, and give them as briefly as possible.

The Creole, Capt. Enson, of Richmond, sailed from that port for New Orleans on the 27th of October, with a cargo of tobacco, four passengers, and one hundred and thirty-five slaves. At 8 o'clock on the evening of Sunday, the 8th ultimo, the Captain supposed himself to be in the vicinity of Abaco, and hove the brig to. At nine o'clock the slaves commenced the attack by shooting Mr. Goddard, the mate, in charge of the deck, with a pistol. The ball slightly wounded him in the back of the head. He made for the cabin, and gave the alarm to the captain and passengers, who had "turned in." The negroes came forward, obstructed the passage from the cabin, exclaiming, "we've got 'em, kill 'em as they come out." Mr. Goddard first rushed out, and, although bruised with clubs and stabbed in one or two places reached the main rigging, and took refuge in the maintop. Capt. Enson followed, and said he was badly stabbed, and thought he was dying. Soon after he fainted, and the mate made him fast to the rigging. A desperate affray took place on deck. Mr. Howell, a passenger, killed one negro with a musket, and fought afterwards like a tiger until he was killed. Several of the sailors fought bravely until they were completely overpowered. The captain and mate remained in the maintop until about five o'clock in the morning, when they were discovered. The ringleaders then ordered them to come down or they would shoot them. Mr. Goddard descended and told them he was at their disposal. One of them presented a musket to his breast, and he was informed he must take them to an English Island, or they would shoot him. He finally assented, and shaped the course of the vessel towards New Providence. Two of the sailors were able to assist him, the others had all been badly wounded in the conflict. In the morning, the captain was taken down, and, with the second mate, Mr. Stevens, the captain's wife, his daughter, four years old, niece, 15 years old, and one of the passengers, confined in the forehold. In the course of the night, the slaves had rifled the vessel, broken open all the trunks, and decked themselves out in such clothing as they could find.

On Tuesday morning, at 8 o'clock, the brig arrived at Nassau. We make the following extract from the letter of Mr. J. T. Bacon, American Consul at Nassau :—

" 'The American Consul, immediately after the arrival of the Creole, had the captain and two of the men taken on shore, and their wounds dressed, and also those on -board, to prevent the slaves from going on shore, he well knowing, if this was not done, it would be impossible to secure those guilty of the murder. This was complied with, and an investigation ordered to be taken by two magistrates. The Consul also has taken testimony of the passengers and crew. Nineteen slaves were identified as having taken an active part in the mutiny and murder, and confined until further orders, the Governor refusing to send them to America for the present, and the remainder of the slaves with the exception of five, were liberated.

Figure 20 American newspaper documenting the actions of fighting slaves.[44]

The explicit details of the countless murders that occurred during these revolts are not provided to glorify violence or incite hatred. They are offered as concrete proof that not all slaves cowered, trembled and cringed in fear of their oppressors, and in some cases potential oppressors, as your common education would have you believe. It is offered as PROOF that SLAVES FOUGHT! These Black men and women meant business. They were going to be free or were going to die and kill trying, period. There was no middle ground and no room for negotiation. Hopefully, the knowledge of their existence balances the negative imagery of SOME slaves prostrating on the ground begging their oppressors to 'have mercy on their po' souls.' The fighting slave said either we will be free as God intended or we will die fighting for our freedom and so will anyone who tries to stop us!

If you're Black, it is undoubtedly invigorating to read the details of YOUR ancestors who stood up for

---

[44] The Daily Picayune, Dec. 3, 1841. 2.

themselves.[45] And those identified in this book only represent the tip of the iceberg. SLAVES FOUGHT! If you so happen to be a descendant of a slave (which not all Black people are because almost a half million Blacks were free in 1860), please know you may be the descendant of one of the previously mentioned or countless other slaves who fought! Slaves fought, slaves fought, SLAVES FOUGHT! Now let's move on to education.

---

[45] If you're not Black, more specifically, if you're the descendant of a European or European American enslaver, the detailed facts of the murder of your people is not meant to offend you. It is simply the rest of his-story that was kept from us all during our primary education.

4 Educated Slaves

"We fully recognize the fact that we are poor and need no weights upon us, and to make our way successfully through life requires thorough organization of the masses, without which our future can not [sp] be a bright one. It is only by our good qualities rightly set forth that we are to succeed in the future. First by educating every boy and girl and teaching from the cradle to the grave honesty, industry, economy of time and means, and the fullest enjoyment of all rights as citizens, and the destruction, death and burial of the accursed idea that the negro is inferior, simply because he has been in time deprived of life, liberty and property. Let us all be wise men and women."

– J. L. Brown as quoted in *Biography and Achievements of the Colored Citizens of Chattanooga, 1904.*[46]

Slaves were educated. Let's repeat that, slaves were educated. Not all, by any stretch of the imagination, but many more than none as your general education would lead you to believe. During your primary education, you learned about the laws that were enacted to prevent slaves from learning and the punishments that were dished out to those who attempted to learn. But have you ever given any deeper thought to those laws?

As you already know, by the time a law is enacted to control any human behavior that behavior is usually already prominent in the society, especially in the United States as

---

[46] J. Bliss White comp. *Biography and Achievements of the Colored Citizens of Chattanooga,* 1904. Reprint, Signal Mountain, TN: Mountain Press, 2004. 13. Mr. J.L. Brown was the great-grandfather of singer Lionel Ritchie as documented in the NBC Series "Who Do You Think You Are", Season 2, Episode 5.

our Legislative system moves slow as molasses. Let's look at an example: cell phone use while driving. How many years had people been driving while using cell phones before individual states started enacting laws outlawing that behavior? In some instances, almost 30 years because it took time for the consequences of that behavior (wrecks and deaths) to prostrate in the general society, then effervesce to lawmakers who then took who knows how long to actually draft and pass the law preventing the behavior. Doesn't it make sense that the exact same process applied to U.S. citizens of the 1800's, especially since they operated under the same Constitution that we do? In order for lawmakers to know educated slaves were a problem, there had to be educated slaves! It's the same process as the cell phone issue in the 21st century: in order for lawmakers to know using cell phones while driving was an issue, people had to have been using the cell phone while driving! Make sense?

Now, the great state of Alabama instituted the following law in 1833: "31. Any person or persons who shall attempt to teach any free person of color, or slave, to spell, read or write, shall upon conviction thereof by indictment, be fined in a sum not less than two hundred and fifty dollars, nor more than five hundred dollars."[47] Now if Alabama instituted the law in 1833, how long prior to 1833 were slaves and FREE persons of color spelling, reading and writing in Alabama? Given slavery started in the early 1600's and ended in 1865, you have to come to the conclusion that plenty of slaves read in the area now known as Alabama before that law was enacted.[48] You can run this drill for other states, as many of them enacted slave code laws at different times, but the point remains: the state would have slaves that knew how to read and write and then some time later would

---

[47] *Digest of the Laws of the State of Alabama*...Philadelphia: Alexander Towar 19 St. James Street, 1833. 397.
[48] Alabama was first settled in 1702 and became a state in 1819.

formally recognize the need to prevent them from learning how to read and write, which all equates to SLAVES WERE EDUCATED!

After the planned Denmark Vesey insurrection was foiled in South Carolina, Charleston residents wrote an appeal to their state politicians. In that 1822 appeal, the citizens of Charleston "recommend that a law be passed, prohibiting under severe penalties, all persons from teaching negroes to read and write"[49] among numerous other restrictions that will be discussed later in the text. So from that request, you can quite logically conclude that some citizens of South Carolina were at some point prior to 1822 teaching Negroes how to read and write! Now, answer this question. Despite the 21st century laws that ban driving while talking and/or texting on the cell phone, how many people do you still see driving while talking and/or texting on the cell phone? Right, plenty! And now WHAT do you think the people, both Black and White, who wanted to educate slaves did? Right, the exact same thing the cell phone users do![50] They still educated slaves despite the law. Because only a fool would believe that a young, LITERATE slave woman (yes, literate slaves existed and we'll get to specific examples shortly) who had her baby in Alabama in 1832 with every intention of teaching that child to read once he/she turned six in 1838, would simply cancel her plans because Alabama outlawed teaching slaves in 1833. Especially not when her Momma taught her and her Big Momma taught her Momma! Logic demands that she STILL would have taught her baby to read, just on the low.

---

[49] *A Documentary History of American Industrial Society vol. II,* 115.
[50] There are complicated formal theories and countless technical terms that can be used to formally confirm this point, which stresses consistency of human behavior across centuries coupled with the colloquialism "laws are made to be broken," but that is not the purpose of this text.

Slaves With Swag

Territory settled by Europeans	Territory becomes a state	State outlaws education of slaves
Slaves being educated ⟶		Slaves **STILL** being educated ⟶

Figure 21 Whether legal or illegal, slaves were educated.

Slaves were educated! Jacobus Capitein was a slave who was very educated. Jacobus was kidnapped near the river St. Andree in Africa around 1724 and given to his enslaver by the slave trader since the trader and the enslaver were friends. Over time, the enslaver moved to Holland where he and Jacobus became friends. Jacobus eventually attended the University of Leyden where he studied for four years and earned a DEGREE! He also published a dissertation in Latin titled *De Vocatione Ethnicorum* and a small volume of sermons in Dutch.[51] Here is Jacobus Capitein:

Figure 22 Jacobus Capitein, an educated slave.

---

[51] Simmons, 1073-77. Wilson Armistead. *A Tribute for the Negro,* Manchester, 1848, 309-12.

Now in case you think Jacobus does not count since there are no cotton fields in Holland and his enslaver was friendly towards him, then please consider Brother Abel. He was an American slave in Virginia who ran away from his enslaver who published the following ad for his capture:

> TWENTY POUNDS REWARD. Run away from the Subscriber, a Mullatto Man named Abel, about forty Years old, near six Feet high, has lost several of his Teeth, large Eyebrows, a Scar or two on some Part of his Face, occasioned by a Brick thrown at him by a Negro, is very apt to stroke his Hand over his Chin, and plays on the Violin. He is well known as a Pilot for York River and the Bay. As I have whipped him twice for his bad Behaviour, I believe Scars may be seen upon his Body. He can write so as to be understood, and once wrote a Pass for a Negro belonging to the Honourable Colonel Corbin, wherein he said the Fellow had served his Time honestly and truly...[52]

And here is a facsimile of the advertisement ran on page 4 of the Jan. 6, 1774 Virginia Gazette:

Figure 23 Facsimile of advertisement for Abel. He was an educated slave who could read and write.

---

[52] Virginia Gazette, Jan. 6, 1774, page 4.

Slaves With Swag

Now Brother Abel was an American slave, and one who lived under particularly harsh conditions given the scars on his face caused by a brick and scars on his body from his enslaver's whip. It is very clear from the advertisement that Brother Abel could read and write exceptionally well. It is also very obvious that his enslaver knew he could read and write very well, so stop making the generalization that slaves were not allowed to read and write! Not only could Brother Abel read and write exceptionally well, but he had the intelligence to write passes for other slaves! And don't you think for one minute that Brother Abel didn't nicely write a pass for himself when he decided to leave! The ad was originally published November 16, 1773 and he was still going strong by January of 1774.

Next we have a dark mulatto slave named Sam. He also ran away and his now former enslaver placed an ad in the February 6, 1755 Maryland Gazette. It read:

RAN away from the Subscriber, the 20th of *November* last, living on *Patuxent* River, near *Upper Marlborough*, in *Prince George's* County, a dark Mulatto Man, named *Sam*, about 5 Feet 9 or 10 Inches high, about 30 Years of Age, a Carpenter by Trade, has a down Look, and low Voice. Had on when he went away, a new Cotton Jacket and Breeches, and Ofnabrigs Shirt; he is fuppofed to have taken with him, one Cotton Coat lined with blue, one red Waiftcoat and Breeches, one blue Silk-Coat, one light Cloth Coat, fome fine Shirts, and one or two good Hats. He is fuppofed to be lurking in *Charles* County, near *Bryan-Town*, where a Mulatto Woman lives, whom he has for fome Time called his Wife; but as he is an artful Fellow, and can read and write, it is probable he may endeavour to make his Efcape out of the Province.

Whoever takes up the faid Runaway, and fecures him fo as his Mafter may get him again, fhall have, if taken out of this Province, Three Pounds; and, if within this Province, Forty Shillings, befides what the Law allows, paid by

William Digges, junior.

Figure 24 The Negro Sam, "an artful fellow" who could "read and write." Facsimile of the Feb. 6, 1755 Maryland Gazette advertisement! [53]

---

[53] The Maryland Gazette, February 6, 1755, 3.

How about John of North Carolina? He also ran away and his advertisement was posted in the Carolina Centinel:

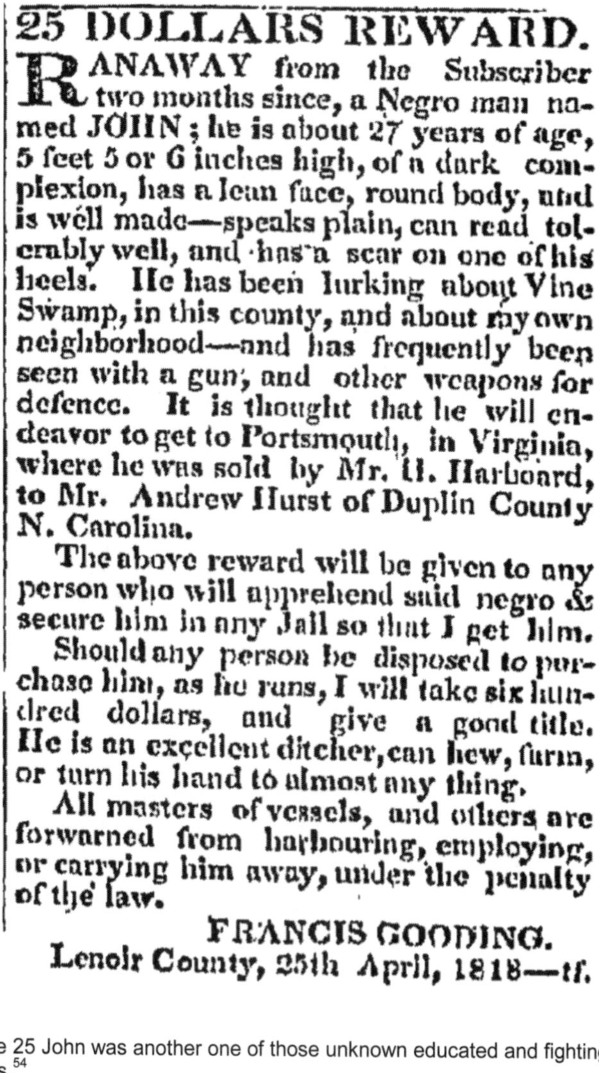

25 DOLLARS REWARD.

RANAWAY from the Subscriber two months since, a Negro man named JOHN; he is about 27 years of age, 5 feet 5 or 6 inches high, of a dark complexion, has a lean face, round body, and is well made—speaks plain, can read tolerably well, and has a scar on one of his heels. He has been lurking about Vine Swamp, in this county, and about my own neighborhood—and has frequently been seen with a gun, and other weapons for defence. It is thought that he will endeavor to get to Portsmouth, in Virginia, where he was sold by Mr. U. Harboard, to Mr. Andrew Hurst of Duplin County N. Carolina.

The above reward will be given to any person who will apprehend said negro & secure him in any Jail so that I get him.

Should any person be disposed to purchase him, as he runs, I will take six hundred dollars, and give a good title. He is an excellent ditcher, can hew, farm, or turn his hand to almost any thing.

All masters of vessels, and others are forewarned from harbouring, employing, or carrying him away, under the penalty of the law.

FRANCIS GOODING.
Lenoir County, 25th April, 1818—tf.

Figure 25 John was another one of those unknown educated and fighting slaves.[54]

The ad specifically states that John "speaks plainly and can read tolerably well." It also states that John has

---

[54] Carolina Centinel, July 11, 1818, 4.

"frequently been seen with a gun or other weapons for defence" which makes John educated and a fighter!

The History curriculum left you with the false impression that slaves were mindless, non-human entities who only served as the pawns of early American settlers. That is not the case. These Black men and women had names (although not their true names), identities, personalities, thoughts, wishes and acted on their own behalf. They fought back, they were educated and you will learn in the coming chapters of this book that they prospered despite their challenges. Remember Nat Turner, who led the insurrection in South Hampton, Virginia? Guess what? He was educated. Thomas B. Gray in his *Confession of Nat Turner,* discusses the grand warrior as follows:

> It has been said he was ignorant and cowardly, and that his object was to murder and rob for the purpose of obtaining money to make his escape. It is notorious, that he was never known to have a dollar in his life; to swear an oath, or drink a drop of spirits. As to his ignorance he certainly never had the advantages of education, but he can read and write, (it was taught him by his parents,) and for natural intelligence and quickness of apprehension, is surpassed by few men I have ever seen.[55]

Thomas B. Gray was a White man who interviewed Nat before his execution. Despite the destruction Mr. Turner and his band of freedom fighters caused, Mr. Gray's honesty resonates, "he can read and write, (it was taught him by his parents,)." So NOT ONLY could Nat read in 1830's Virginia, his PARENTS could read as well a generation earlier! He was a slave that could read and write AND had slave parents who obviously cared for him and raised him! You thought all slaves were ripped from the bosom of their mother at birth! No Sir, no Ma'am, not the case. Mr. Gray continues, "and for natural intelligence and quickness of apprehension, [Nat Turner][56] is surpassed by few men I have ever seen." Listen to this White man's compliment of a Black 'rebel' slave!

---

[55] Gray, 18.
[56] Parenthetical comment added by the author for clarity.

Joseph E. Jones was born a slave in Lynchburg, Virginia on October 15, 1850. His mother was of the firm belief that all slaves would be freed one day and didn't mind telling other slaves and her own enslaver what she thought.[57] To prepare her son for freedom, she "secured the services" of a fellow slave named Robert A. Perkins to teach young Joseph to read and write. When the enslaver found out, they retaliated by selling off Robert, but that did not discourage Mrs. Jones. From there she paid an ill Confederate soldier by feeding him in exchange for an education for her son. After the war was over and the slaves freed, Joseph's original teacher, Robert Perkins opened a private school that Joseph attended. As a man, Joseph E. Jones would become PROFESSOR Jones at the Theological Seminary in Richmond, Virginia where he taught Homiletics and Greek.[58] Here is a picture of Professor Jones who received his early education from a fellow slave and sick confederate soldier thanks to his mother:

Figure 26 Ex-slave turned Professor Joseph E. Jones.

---

[57] Simmons, 234-5.
[58] Simmons, 234-9. Charles H Corey. *A History of the Richmond Theological Seminary. Richmond:* J.W. Randolph Company. 1895. 174-8.

Slaves With Swag

John Oliver Crosby was an educated slave. He was born a slave on December 22, 1850 at Crosbyville, Fairfield County, South Carolina. Dr. Simmons notes that John Oliver "was to the boys on the plantation what 'Webster's Dictionary' is to the learned."[59] John was one of those slaves who was separated from his mother, but after the war John, his younger brother and mother reunited. Unfortunately, John did not get along with his step-father, so he and his little brother headed to Winnsboro with nothing but a pound of bacon and some ash cake. To make a long story short, John worked hard during the day to support his brother, went to school at night and eventually earned a Bachelor's degree from Shaw University in 1874. He eventually became an ordained minister and earned a DOCTOR of Philosophy degree from Shaw University in 1891. And just a year later in 1892, Dr. John Oliver Crosby became the first President of North Carolina A&T University.[60] Here is a picture of Dr. Crosby:

Figure 27 John Oliver Crosby. From slave to Doctor of Philosophy to first President of North Carolina A&T.

---

[59] Simmons, 424.
[60] Simmons, 422-7. A.W. Pegues. Our Baptist Ministers and Schools. Springfield: Wiley & Co. 1892. 137-43.

And there are more, many more! Elijah P. Marrs was an educated slave. Elijah was born in January of 1840 in Shelby County, Kentucky. His mother was a slave of Jesse Robinson, but his Black father was NOT a slave at all! (In other words, Elijah's father was a Category 3 pre-1865 Black man). But since children followed the plight of their mother, Elijah was a slave when born. In his autobiography Elijah explains how he came to read and write while still a slave. He wrote:

> Very early in life I took up the idea that I wanted to learn to read and write. I was convinced that there would be something for me to do in the future that I could not accomplish by remaining in ignorance. I had heard so much about freedom, and of the colored people running off and going to Canada, that my mind was busy with this subject even in my young days. I sought the aid of the white boys, who did all they could in teaching me. They did not know that it was dangerous for a slave to read and write. I availed myself of every opportunity, daily I carried my book in my pocket, and every chance that offered would be learning my A, B, C's. Soon I learned to read. After this the white people would send me daily to the post-office, at Simpsonville, Ky., a distance of two miles, when I would read the address of the letters; I also would read the newspapers the best I could. There was an old colored man on the place by the name of Ham Graves, who opened a night school, beginning at 10 o'clock at night. I attended his school one year and learned how to write my name and read writing. On every gate - post around the stable, as on the plowhandles, you could see where I had been trying to write.[61]

William J. Simmons explains in *Men of Mark* that after Elijah learned to read well, "he devoured the contents of newspapers and books, and being the only colored man, except his brother, H. C. (now deceased), in the neighborhood who could read, he kept the colored people in the community well informed on the state of affairs."[62] Slaves were E-D-U-C-A-T-E-D! Dr. Simmons also highlighted the fighting spirit of Mr. Marrs in the following account:

---

[61] Elijah Marrs. *Life and History of Rev. Elijah P. Marrs, First Pastor of Beargrass Baptist Church, and Author.* Louisville: Bradley & Gilbert Co., 1885. 11-2. Also available online as part of the University of North Carolina digitization project at http://docsouth.unc.edu/neh/marrs/marrs.html.
[62] Simmons, 579-80.

Slaves With Swag

Shelby county was threatened with Confederate soldiers, and his former master warned him to be on the alert and not be captured; but though heeding the caution given, he mustered a company of twenty-seven men, Sunday night, September 25, 1864, armed them with clubs, and as their captain, armed himself with an old pistol which had long discharged its last shot, marched a distance of twenty-two miles to Louisville and enlisted in the United States army. Two days later he was made a sergeant of Company L, Twelfth United States Heavy Artillery.[63]

After the war, Mr. Marrs became a Reverend and a teacher. Ultimately, he helped establish and became the first President of the Kentucky Baptist Normal and Theological Institute which was later renamed to the State University of Kentucky and ultimately named Simmons College of Kentucky! Yes, the same Simmons College of Kentucky that was named after Dr. Simmons! Mr. Marrs was the first President and Dr. Simmons was the second. It wasn't renamed Simmons College of Kentucky until after Dr. Simmons' tenure was over. Here is a picture of the gentlemen Rev. Elijah P. Marrs:

Figure 28 Reverend Elijah P. Marrs. From slave to first President of what is now known as Simmons College of Kentucky.

---

[63] Simmons, 580.

4 Educated Slaves

Newell Houston Ensley was an educated slave. Newell's enslaver was his mother's father who wanted all his slaves to be educated. Therefore, this grandfather/enslaver hired a teacher to teach his slaves, including his grandson Newell, to read and write. In this particular case, not only was Newell an educated slave, but all the slaves on that particular plantation were educated, including Newell's parents George and Clara Ensley. After slavery, Newell attended Roger Williams University and taught at Howard University and Alcorn University. Here is a picture of Professor Newell Houston Ensley[64]:

Figure 29 Educated slave Newell Houston Ensley.

Frank Grimke was born a slave in Charleston, South Carolina on November 4, 1850, but wasn't educated until after he was freed. Frank is one of those slaves whose father and enslaver was one in the same man. His mother was a

---

[64] Simmons, 361-7.

slave and in those days, the child followed the plight of the mother, so Frank was born a slave. When Frank was still a boy, his father/enslaver died which left Frank and his other siblings in the care of Frank's oldest half-brother E. Montague Grimke.

Initially, E. Montague provided good care for Frank and his enslaved siblings, but when Frank got to be about ten years-old, Montague decided to profit off his younger siblings unfortunate status as 'slaves' and put Frank and crew to work. Now, its one thing to be enslaved by your father, but a whole other thing to be enslaved by a brother and Frank wasn't having it. He ran away and joined the Union Army, but unfortunately was captured by his brother. Montague, fearing Frank would flee again, sold Frank to an officer of the Union Army who employed Frank as a soldier until the close of the war. Frank was only about 15.

After attending the Morris Street School in Charleston, the Principal of the school, Mrs. Pillsbury, arranged for Frank and another brother, Archibald Grimke, to be sent North for an education. Frank eventually attended Lincoln University near Philadelphia and was an outstanding student. He graduated in 1870 VALEDICTORIAN of his class. After briefly studying Law at Lincoln University and Howard University, Frank was inspired to be a man of God and enrolled in the Princeton Theological Seminary which he graduated in 1878. Reverend Frank Grimke served as pastor of the 15th Street Presbyterian Church in the District of Columbia and then the Laurel Street Presbyterian Church in Jacksonville, Florida.[65] When the citizens of D.C. heard Rev. Grimke may leave for Jacksonville, one of them sent the following letter to the Washington Bee newspaper which, by-the-way, was owned and edited by a FREE Black man named William Calvin Chase (another Category 3 Brother):

[65] Simmons, 608-12.

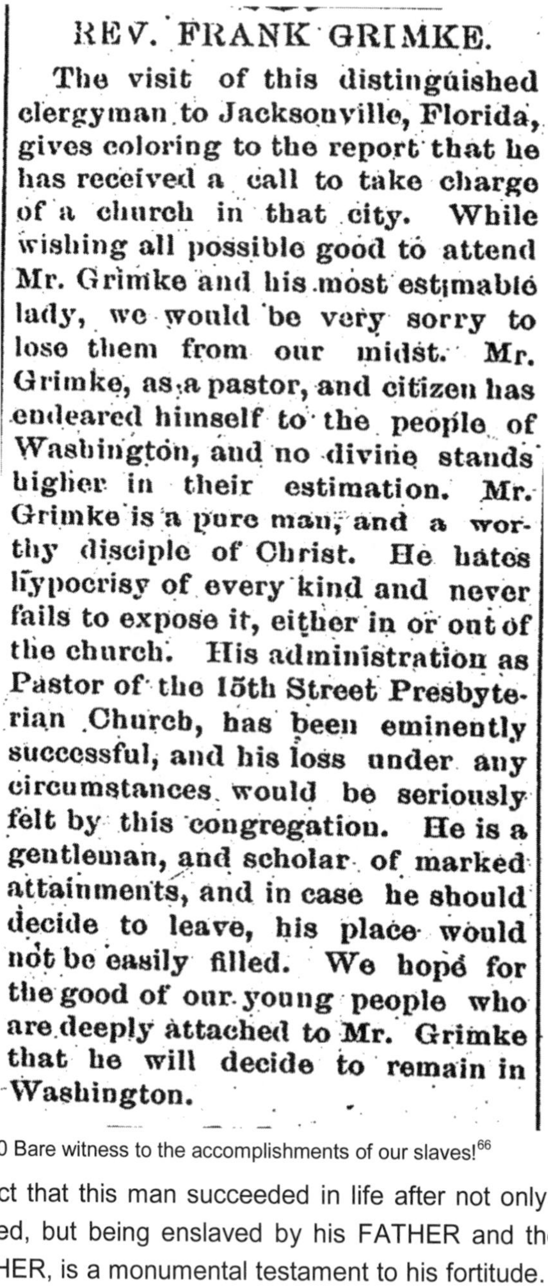

REV. FRANK GRIMKE.

The visit of this distinguished clergyman to Jacksonville, Florida, gives coloring to the report that he has received a call to take charge of a church in that city. While wishing all possible good to attend Mr. Grimke and his most estimable lady, we would be very sorry to lose them from our midst. Mr. Grimke, as a pastor, and citizen has endeared himself to the people of Washington, and no divine stands higher in their estimation. Mr. Grimke is a pure man, and a worthy disciple of Christ. He hates hypocrisy of every kind and never fails to expose it, either in or out of the church. His administration as Pastor of the 15th Street Presbyterian Church, has been eminently successful, and his loss under any circumstances would be seriously felt by this congregation. He is a gentleman, and scholar of marked attainments, and in case he should decide to leave, his place would not be easily filled. We hope for the good of our young people who are deeply attached to Mr. Grimke that he will decide to remain in Washington.

Figure 30 Bare witness to the accomplishments of our slaves![66]

The fact that this man succeeded in life after not only being enslaved, but being enslaved by his FATHER and then his BROTHER, is a monumental testament to his fortitude. And if

---

[66] Washington Bee, Apr. 4, 1885. 2.

Slaves With Swag

he was able to gain an education and enact his skill in a positive manner despite his challenges as not only a Black man but a Black ex-slave in mid-to-late 1800's, then you should be able to achieve even more in the 21st century. Let's admire our next educated slave.

Dr. Anthony William Amo (also known as Anton Wilhelm Amo) was another educated man of African descent. He, like Jacobus Capitein, was kidnapped from Africa and taken to Europe. Amo was kidnapped from Guinea, Africa in the early 1700's and ultimately taken to Germany. Once in Germany, he was befriended and duly educated at the University of Halle and the University of Wittenberg. In 1734, he earned a Ph.D from the University of Wittenberg and went on to become a professor.[67]

Mr. John W. Stephenson was an educated slave/servant. John was born in Baltimore, Maryland about 1836 to John and Ann Stephenson. When John was about four years-old, his parents "removed" the family, including John and his five other siblings, to Trinidad. A year later his father died and his mother was forced to bring the family back to Baltimore where John was "bound out"[68] to labor on a farm outside the city. He was sold four different times before he turned 19 and made his way to Philadelphia. Once in Philadelphia, John became a porter in a drug store owned by Henry Kollock on the corner of 9th and Chestnut streets where the following took place:

> Mr. William Kearney and his brother, clerks in the store, observing the extraordinary talent which Mr. Stephenson exhibited, commenced to instruct him in medicine. In one year he had made such progress in compounding that he was made a clerk in the store. Mr. Kollock desiring that he should become a physician for his people, sent him to Dr. Wilson, a colored physician practicing in the city, that he might receive the necessary instruction from an able doctor of his own race. It not

[67] Simmons, 617-9. Armistead, 265-7.
[68] From analyzing the data, it seems John was a servant rather than a slave, the difference being servants served for a period of time rather than their entire lives. Servitude was much more prominent among poor White families than Black ones, but in this case John Stephenson was a Black servant.

being convenient for Dr. Wilson to take him at the time, by the influence of his friends, he was received by Professor Woodward, with whom he remained five years, engaged in his professional studies at the Philadelphia University of Medicine.[69]

Dr. Stephenson practiced medicine in many areas of the northeast United States including around Lincoln University where he also was a student for a few years. In addition to practicing medicine, the good doctor also did a significant amount of raising funds for and erecting numerous churches.[70] SLAVES WERE EDUCATED!

Rufus L. Perry was born a slave in Tennessee to parents Lewis and Maria Perry who were enslaved by one Archibald W. Overton. Despite being a slave, Rufus' father was a skilled mechanic, carpenter and cabinet maker. Due to Lewis' skills, he and his family lived with unprecedented freedom to include the formal schooling of young Rufus, who attended a school for FREE Black children in Tennessee up until his father escaped to Canada. After his father's escape, the rest of the family, to include young Rufus, was sent to the plantation to slave where Rufus remained until his escape to Canada about 1852. A few years later, Rufus returned to the U.S. to attend the Kalamazoo Seminary in Kalamazoo, Michigan where he proudly graduated with the Class of 1861. After graduation, Mr. Perry was the Pastor of several churches including the Second Baptist Church in Ann Arbor, Michigan and St. Catherine's Church in Buffalo, New York. Dr. Simmons says Mr. Perry "is fluent graceful and earnest" as a preacher in addition to being a "very logical, clear reasoner, close and active debater, deep thinker and an excellent writer."[71]

---

[69] Simmons, 821.
[70] Benjamin T. Tanner. An *Apology for African Methodism*. Benjamin T. Tanner. Baltimore. 1867. 183-8. Also available online as part of the University of North Carolina digitization project at http://docsouth.unc.edu/church/tanner/tanner.html.
[71] Simmons, 621.

Slaves With Swag

When the rest of the slaves were freed in 1865, Mr. Perry played an important role in educating them, specifically the significance of their African History when he wrote *The Cushite, or the Children of Ham as seen by the Ancient Historians and Poets.* In *The Cushite* Mr. Perry wrote:

From what has been shown, there is sufficient warrant for the conclusion:

1. That the ancient Cushite, the progenitor of the modern Negro, led the world for centuries in all that related to civilization and human progress. To this fact the holy scriptures bear testimony in saying (Acts vii. 22) that "Moses was learned in all the wisdom of the Egyptians, and was mighty in words and in deeds." This Egyptian learning came into Egypt from Ethiopia and went from Egypt into other parts of the world.

2. That the art of war, that prowess in man hunting inaugurated by Nimrod in the land of Shinar, soon reappeared in Ethiopia and, descending the Nile into Lower Egypt, there, as in Ethiopia, formed itself into a kind of military academy for the world, and subsequently sent out a Sesostris terrible in war, and a Shishak as skilled and brave as any general of the ancient Asiatic or European nations; or as any of the nineteenth century, not excepting Napoleon in Europe or Washington in America.

3. That the art of writing, originating first in pictorial symbols and then developing into phonetic characters, was imported by the Cushite priests of Ethiopia into Egypt; and from there they found their way to Phoenicia, Mesopotamia, Greece and other countries, finally returning to Egypt an alphabet of finer finish.

4. That religious thought, civil law, mechanical art and the science of medicine were all of like origin.

The art of embalming the dead was a special department of medical science in which the Cushite physicians of Egypt excelled. Their embalming was so skillfully done that even now, after a lapse of more than three thousand years, it remains a witness to their scientific knowledge.

5. That, looking back over the centuries from the Christian era to Noah, and noting the rise and fall of great men and great nations, we see none more conspicuous than the children of Ham.

Greece had her Athens, and could boast of Homer, Herodotus, Plato, Solon, Socrates, and Demosthenes, and a host of other poets, historians, philosophers and orators, and of her great Alexander. Persia had her Cyrus the Great, her Cambyses, her Darius and her religious Zoroaster; China had her great cities walled in so that nothing could come in or go out but the theosophic philosophy of her deified Confucius; Rome had her noted patricians, and, like Greece, her poets, orators, historians and generals, and begat for herself a great name; but before all these is the land of Ham, of Cush and the Cushite; the land chosen of God in which to train his peculiar people, and as a city of refuge for His own Son when Herod sought to slay him.

Africa had her Cushite Meroe, her Thebes, her Memphis, her sciences and her wonderful works of art; she had a great commercial traffic with the nations of the East, borne from country to country by numerous caravans. She had her high priests, whose sacred hieroglyphics bespoke their reverence for their gods. She had a thousand thousand soldiers, infantry and cavalry, with generals of unequalled prowess; she had her astronomers, physicians, and wise men,—men of deeds rather than of words, of actions rather than of theory. She had her Sesostris, her Memnon, her Shishak, her Zerah, her Nitocris, her Queen of Sheba, her Candaces, and her long line of great Pharaohs mentioned in the sacred Scriptures.[72]

The way you were taught doesn't even allow you to fathom the existence of an ex-slave who could not only write, but write eloquently while educating his fellow ex-slaves on the African Origin of Human Civilization! Absolutely astounding! On May 18, 1887, Mr. Perry gave the commencement address at the State University of Kentucky graduation ceremony (now known as Simmons College of Kentucky), after which the University conferred upon him a Ph.D. in Philosophy. Dr. Perry eventually settled in Brooklyn, New York. He was an educated slave!

Figure 31 Rev. Dr. Rufus L. Perry, an educated slave.

[72] Rev. Rufus L. Perry. *The Cushite or the Descendants of Ham as Found in the Sacred Scriptures and in the Writings of Ancient Historian and Poets From Noah to the Christian Era*. Springfield, MA: Wiley & Co., 1893. 158-160. Simmons, 620-5.

Slaves With Swag

J.J. Durham was an educated slave. J.J. was born April 13, 1849 in Spartanburg County, South Carolina and remained a slave until the end of the Civil War. During his slave years, J.J. served as an apprentice to a blacksmith and learned how to read and write during any spare time he had. When slavery was over, young J.J. went on an educational rampage. Between 1873 and 1880, Mr. Durham attended the South Carolina College, Atlanta University and Fisk University in Nashville, Tennessee. And in May of 1880 he graduated from Fisk University with a Bachelor's degree thanks to his hard work, $50 given to him by his father and a $20 per month scholarship received from the state of South Carolina. J.J. always had an urge to preach the word of God and was initially licensed to preach in 1867. Now formally educated, he returned to Columbia, South Carolina and became Pastor of the Nazareth Baptist Church.

While tending to the souls' of his fellow man, Mr. Durham couldn't help but recognize the poor condition of some of their bodies, so he went back to school to study medicine at the Meharry Medical College in Nashville, Tennessee. Meharry Medical College is a private Historically Black College and University that started as the Medical Department of Central Tennessee College of Nashville in 1876. When Central Tennessee became Walden in 1915, Meharry Medical College became its own entity. Meharry has been educating Black Doctors and Dentists since 1876 and Dr. J.J. Durham was VALEDICTORIAN of its graduating class of 1882! Dr. Durham went on to be a successful Doctor of Medicine and Pastor.[73] He was a founding member of Morris College in Sumter, South Carolina and was absolutely an

---

[73] Rev. Durham was the sixth Pastor of the Second African Baptist Church in Savannah, Georgia. The church is still located at 123 Houston Street in Savannah. If you live close by, go there and see the stone commemorating the church's centennial in 1902 when Rev. Durham was Pastor. It states "Second African Baptist Church, Constituted Dec 26.1802., Rev. J.J. Durham. A.M.M.D.D.D., 6th Pastor." This tangible reference will reinforce the knowledge of this man's existence.

educated slave.[74] Here is a picture of the great Dr. and Pastor J.J. Durham:

Figure 32 Dr. Rev. J.J. Durham from *Our Baptist Ministers and Schools* *which was* written by another Black man named Dr. Rev. A.W. Pegues.

Now how many of these great men have you heard of before reading this book? Truth is, you probably knew absolutely nothing about any of them and even less than nothing (if that's possible) about their illustrious Black educators, most of whom were born free. For example, William H. Gibson was born to FREE parents in Baltimore, Maryland. And even though he was born in a slave state in the early 1800's, William H. Gibson was never a slave! His parent's names were Phillip and Amelia Gibson. The records do not state how Phillip and Amelia were free, but it does say that "they gave him [William] all the advantages of an education, that the city of his birth offered to the Negro child, and in 1834, when he was but five years of age, he could read. Continuing his studies, he had for several years as instructor John Fortie, a prominent teacher."[75] When William

---

[74] Simmons, 878-82. Pegues, 183-7. "A Record of the Darker Races," *The Crisis*, March 1921, 227.
[75] Simmons, 545.

was 18, he moved to Louisville, Kentucky and with the help of Rev. James Harper and Robert Lane, he opened a school in the basement of the Methodist Church on the corner of 4th and Green Streets. And in that basement classroom, Mr. Gibson taught "hundreds of slaves, holding written permissions from their masters" along with "the free children."[76] But up until this point, you were unaware of those educated slaves, free Blacks and their great educator Mr. Gibson who is pictured below:

Figure 33 William Gibson who was born a FREE Black man in Baltimore and moved to Louisville, KY to teach slaves and free Black children.

Mr. Gibson represents just one of the thousands of Black educators of slaves! Mr. Ham Graves, mentioned in Elijah P. Marrs' autobiography, was another one of those educators.[77] The men identified in this chapter are just a handful of hundreds of thousands of their slave students who were educated! Don't you believe for one second every pre-1865 Black person was a 'yessum boss, I'se gittin' it raght now' type, because you just read of several who were not. So

---

[76] Horace Talbert. *The Sons of Allen: Together with a Sketch of the Rise and Progress of Wilberforce University, Wilberforce, Ohio.* Xenia, OH: Aldine Press, 1906. 102.

[77] If you missed his name, please go back and re-read the history of Elijah P. Marrs earlier in this chapter. The old colored gentlemen Mr. Graves, who educated slaves in Shelby County, KY in the mid-1800's deserves homage.

in your next conversation about slavery when someone blindly throws out some undocumented fact about all slaves being ignorant or 'you know slaves weren't allowed to read', it is your duty to respectfully correct them with the truth, the documented truth! Slaves were educated, that is a fact. The final piece of evidence for this point comes from a slave named Olaudah Equiano. Olaudah was kidnapped from New Guinea, Africa in the mid-1700's, brought to Virginia to slave, then sold to a ship Captain. After spending some time in less strenuous conditions on the ship, Olaudah wrote the following passage about the feeling he had when re-approaching land and a plantation from the sea:

> At the sight of this land of bondage, a fresh horror ran through all my frame, and chilled me to the heart. My former slavery now rose in dreadful review to my mind, and displayed nothing but misery, stripes, and chains; and, in the first paroxysm of my grief, I called upon God's thunder, and his avenging power, to direct the stroke of death to me, rather than permit me to become a slave, and be sold from lord to lord.[78]

You see Olaudah eventually purchased his freedom from his final slaver and wrote a couple hundred page autobiography titled *The Interesting Narrative of the Life of Olaudah Equiano or Gustavus Vassa, The African, Written by Himself.* The above passage was quoted from this book. It is provided as a demonstration of intellectual prowess of slaves. After all, the man used the word paroxysm[79] in the late 1700s! Here is our stately Brother, Olaudah Equiano a.k.a. Gustavus Vassa:

---

[78] Olaudah Equiano. *The Interesting Narrative of the Life of Olaudah Equiano or Gustavus Vassa, The African. Written By Himself. 9th ed.* London: Olaudah Equiano, 1789. 123-4.
[79] Now be honest, how many of you even knew how to pronounce paroxysm, nevertheless its meaning? But don't fret, just get your dictionary and look it up like I did.

Figure 34 Educated slave Olaudah Equiano.

Slaves were educated! Slaves were educated! SLAVES WERE EDUCATED!

5 Slaves With Freedom & Money

A certain negro woman was manumitted in 1823, and a few years after bought several acres of land, the deed for which was properly executed and recorded.
-Jeffrey R. Brackett Ph.D., *The Negro in Maryland, 1889.* [80]

In case you read the title of this chapter as a question (Slaves With Freedom & Money?) instead of a statement, the answer is YES, SLAVES HAD FREEDOM AND MONEY! Sounds like an oxymoron, huh? Jargon wise it may be, but in reality, these people existed. Don't believe it? Let's get to it.

The good people of 1822 South Carolina left some documentation that proves slaves had freedom and money. As mentioned earlier in the book, a Black man named Denmark Vesey planned a grand revolt in Charleston, South Carolina in 1822. The revolt was quelled before it was executed, but the intricacies and extensiveness of the planning was so impressive, it frightened the Whites of the area. It frightened them so much so that the White citizens of Charleston compiled a memorial (a petition) to the South Carolina Senate and House of Representatives in an attempt to get their Negroes back in line. Of the plot, the petition read "whilst the citizens were reposing the utmost confidence in the fidelity of the negroes, the latter were plotting the destruction of the former. A plan was perfected – a corps was organized – arms were collected, and everything arranged to

---

[80] Jeffrey Brackett, *The Negro in Maryland, A Study of the Institution of Slavery.* Baltimore: Johns Hopkins University, 1889. 164.

overwhelm us with calamity..."[81] What this short passage proves is that slaves fought (but you already know that by now) and had the freedom to organize. You thought slaves only woke up at the crack of dawn, ate some mush, slaved all day until the dinner bell rang, ate more mush, went to sleep only to wake up and do it all over again. Does that represent the daily routine of SOME slaves? Sure, but not all. The citizens who wrote the petition clarify:

> ...the owners of slaves in our state were rearing up a system, which extended many privileges to our negroes; afforded them greater protection; relieved them from numerous restraints; enabled them to assemble without the presence of a white person for the purpose of social intercourse or religious worship; yielding to them the facilities of acquiring most of the comforts and many of the luxuries of improved society; and what is of more importance, affording them means of enlarging their minds and extending their information[82]

Now, the last sentence in the quote reinforces the fact that slaves were educated. But the rest of the quote introduces you to the concept that slaves had freedom! The citizens used words that are hard to argue with such as 'privileges', 'protection', 'enabled', 'comforts', and 'luxuries'. Slaves had freedom people.

Even Denmark Vesey himself was a slave with enormous freedom. Denmark was pulled from a shipment of 390 slaves from St. Thomas and made a pet of the ship's Captain, Captain Vesey. Captain Vesey was a slave trader who made his living shipping slaves between St. Thomas and Cape Francois in San Domingo, Haiti. When the Captain got bored with Denmark, he sold him off during one of his trips to Haiti. When Captain Vesey returned to Haiti, Denmark's purchaser asked for and received a refund as Denmark was somewhat sickly. Now, here's where the freedom part comes in. Denmark was a slave for the first 38 years of his life until the year 1800 when he PLAYED AND HIT THE EAST BAY

[81] *A Documentary History of American Industrial Society vol. II*, 104.
[82] *A Documentary History of American Industrial Society vol. II*, 103-4.

STREET LOTTERY![83] DENMARK WON $1,500 IN 1822, WHICH IS THE EQUIVALENT OF ABOUT $25,000 IN TODAY'S CURRENCY! And what did Denmark do with his cash? He took $600 of it and purchased himself from his enslaver! Don't believe it?! Here is an exact facsimile of the September 9, 1822 Connecticut Herald article about the insurrection that gave some history on Denmark Vesey.

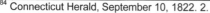

> long maturing, and was deep and deadly. The ringleader and most active agent in this projected rebellion, was a free black, by the name of *Denmark Vesey*. This fellow was taken by a Captain Vesey, among other slaves, in 1781, and sold at Cape Francois; he was then 14 years of age, which would make him, at the present time, 55 years. The captain was obliged to take him back, on his being pronounced unsound, and for 20 years Vesey was his faithful, honest slave. In 1800, Vesey drew a prize of $1,500 in the Lottery, and purchased his freedom. He subsequently worked at the carpenter's trade; was a powerful black, bold, despotic and ambitious. He could read and write with facility, and appears to have been the sole mover and instigator of the plot.

Figure 35 Connecticut Herald article that clearly documents Denmark Vesey was playing the lottery as a slave in 1822 South Carolina! Other articles called out the East Bay Street Lottery specifically.[84]

If you read the article closely, you would have noticed that in addition to being a 1) fighter, 2) having freedom, and money, Mr. Vesey was also 3) EDUCATED! The article clearly states that "…he was a powerful black, bold, despotic and ambitious. He could read and write with facility…" Now without reading this undeniable proof for yourself, how many of you would have believed a slave would have not only played the lottery, but hit then got to keep his jackpot for himself?! And who would have thought that slave would then use that jackpot to purchase his own freedom from his former enslaver?! NONE! Why? The curriculum you were taught

[83] James Hamilton. *Negro Plot. An Account of the Late Intended Insurrection Among a Portion of the Blacks of the City of Charleston, South Carolina* 2*nd* ed. Boston: Joseph W. Ingraham, 1822. 17. Also available online as part of the University of North Carolina digitization project at http://docsouth.unc.edu/church/church/Hamilton/Hamilton.html.
[84] Connecticut Herald, September 10, 1822. 2.

under left you to assume all slaves were docile, submissive, obedient, meek and meager. And while SOME were, many were not. You need to know the rest of the story to have a true knowledge of yourself. You need the rest of the story to know your true value. You need to know about Brother Denmark. He didn't cower in front of his enslaver. He approached him, like a man. His chin was up, chest was out, he could read and write, and undoubtedly was full with a sense of rebellion attained from his time in Haiti, land of the greatest revolutionary Toussaint L'Overture. Denmark's numbers finally hit and his pockets were filled with money and he negotiated an excellent price to PURCHASE HIS FREEDOM! And most of you knew nothing about him! Slaves had freedom and money!

Denmark wasn't the only slave with freedom and money. In *The Negro in Maryland,* Jeffrey Bracket states "not a few slaves in Maryland, particularly, in the cities, were allowed by their masters to live and act as freemen, and also to buy their own freedom by their extra earnings."[85] Apparently it was a regular occurrence for the slaves of Charleston to walk the street in fine apparel as the petitioners stated the "object is to prevent the slaves from wearing silks, satins, crepes, lace muslins and such costly stuffs, as are looked upon as considered the luxury of dress."[86]

A Documentary History of American Industrial Society quoted other White citizens of Athens, Georgia who wrote into a local newspaper about threat of slave insurrections in their area. The article titled 'Negro Insurrection' read:

> NEGRO INSURRECTION. We believe our citizens have generally recovered from the "fright" into which some of them were thrown by the report that an attempt at insurrection was to be made by the negroes throughout the South during the Christmas holidays. We were not amongst those who apprehended any danger. First, because the great mass of

---

[85] Brackett, 106-7.
[86] *A Documentary History of American Industrial Society vol. II*, 116-7.

the negroes are well treated and are so much "better off" than the whites, that they have no excuse for making such an attempt; and, secondly, because they in common with the whites, know that the present state of affairs is better for the interest of both races; and furthermore, that an attempt at insurrection would not only signally fail of its object, but result in the immediate massacre of every African concerned in it.

While on this subject, it may not be improper to remark that negroes enjoy too much latitude here. We would not abridge one iota of their comforts, but most of them enjoy greater freedom than their masters...[87]

While some points in the article may be somewhat offensive, its overall theme is undeniable. The author is saying they're not worried about slaves in their area revolting because most of them are "better off than the whites" and "enjoy greater freedom than their masters." Please note this article wasn't written by some historian 50 or 100 years after the fact. It was published January 1, 1857 in the Southern Watchman newspaper in Athens, Georgia by someone who lived in the era! Slaves had freedom and money! The slaves in Maryland had so much freedom that it was brought up as an issue in the Maryland Legislature in 1787 and 1802. The Maryland House Journals for both of those years recorded the endorsement of a bill to prevent slaves from acting as free. The 1787 Journal stated:[88]

Which were read.
And also a bill, entitled, An act to prevent the inconveniences arising from slaves being permitted to act as free, endorsed; " By the senate, May 10, 1787: Read the first time and ordered to lie on " the table.
                                    " By order,   J. DORSEY, clk.
" By the senate, May 10, 1787: Read the second time by especial order and will pass.
                                    " By order,   J. DORSEY, clk."

And the 1802 Journal stated:[89]

                                    " By order,   J. B. DUCKETT, clk."
And a bill, entitled, An act to prevent slaves hiring themselves, or acting as free, and to repeal the act of assembly therein mentioned, endorsed; " By the senate, November 18, 1802: Read the first time and ordered to lie on the table.
                                    " By order,   J. B. DUCKETT, clk.
" By the senate, December 3, 1802: Read the second time and will pass.

---

[87] A Documentary History of American Industrial Society vol. II, 116-7.
[88] Maryland House Journal, May 10, 1787. 150.
[89] House Journal, December 3, 1802, 43.

Slaves With Swag

Now if lawmakers finally got around to addressing slaves acting as freemen in 1787, then those Brothers and Sisters had already been acting in that manner for a while. And like the cell phone example, they continued to act as such despite the law because it was addressed again in 1802!

In late December 1858, several Black men were arrested in Baltimore as runaways. When they were taken to trial it was discovered that they came to Baltimore to spend the Christmas holiday. Their passes were accidently left on the boat that brought them there. They were brought before the judge and eventually released by the Superior Court![90] Slaves travelled on the holidays! In fact, not only did they travel, but they also took advantage of the early commercialization of American holidays. Bracket states in *The Negro in Maryland* that "On Saturday afternoons, some slaves had less than usual work to do, and it was the general custom to give holidays at Christmas and Easter-tide." Bracket continued to explain that "the market places of the county towns might be thronged with blacks" on those days.[91]

The Blacks weren't at the markets to slave! They went to the market places as both SELLERS and BUYERS of goods! How in the world did they do that, might you ask? Easily, let's break it down. A field slave would grow crops on a plantation from about April through the fall harvest, which accounts for roughly 7 months out of the year. What do you suppose the slave did the other 5 months? Sat around and did nothing at all but eat off his enslaver? No way. Many slaves were allotted a small piece of land with which to grow their own food and raise their own chickens. If they were able to produce more than they needed to feed themselves and their families, they would take the excess goods to market to SELL. Brackett clarifies:

---

[90] Brackett, 90.
[91] Brackett, 104.

Generally, the slave had at least a garden and chicken coop, from whose proceeds he got such luxuries as coffee and tobacco. Some masters bought what the slaves raised-even at the risk, occasionally, of paying for a sweet potato or a chicken that was already theirs; others gave their slaves permits to sell and buy; others, still, lay asleep in the big house, while the black quietly did his bartering at some corner store or on some boat in the river.[92]

So now you know how slaves went to market as sellers, let's move on to the buying piece.

Countless slaves were allowed to 'hire themselves out', which means they were allowed to work for other people for MONEY even though they were slaves. The Statutes at Large of Pennsylvania 1725-26 contained the following law:

[Section XI] And be it enacted by the authority aforesaid, That no master or mistress of any negro shall hereafter for any reward, sum or sums of money stipulated and agreed upon betwixt them or upon any other pretense whatsoever permit or suffer his or their negroes to ramble about under pretense of getting work, give liberty to their negroes to seek their own employ and so go to work at their own wills, under the penalty of twenty shillings for every such offense.[93]

And again, if the law was written in 1725, the practice was taking place some years before then. So why would an enslaver allow his slave to "go work at their own wills" for another person for money? Simple, the same reason he/she would allow the slave to grow their own food, it was cheaper. If a slave had no other means of eating, then the enslaver had to feed the slave year round, whether the slave was making money for the enslaver or not. So, the enslaver would allow the slave to hire himself out, i.e. meaning find work in other places, during the times when there was no work for him/her to do on the plantation. Allowing a slave to hire himself out meant less sustainment costs for the enslaver! And on top of the saved costs of having to feed the slave, the enslaver would sometimes get a percentage of the slaves' earnings as well. Make sense? Good.

---

[92] Brackett, 104.

[93] *The Statutes at Large of Pennsylvania from 1682 to 1801, vol. IV 1724 to 1744.* Pennsylvania: 1897. 63-4.

Slaves With Swag

Now, what the enslaver miscalculated was the talent, skill and innovation of Black people. What the enslaver soon found out was that many of the slaves were talented. The community at large discovered slaves were talented as well and there was a high demand for their goods and services, despite limited resources. The slaves weren't just talented laborers. No, no, no, they were well sought after skilled craftsman who made a pretty penny from their efforts. Some of them were able to save their money and amass small fortunes from their hiring out endeavors. And what do you think the slaves did with these small fortunes? If you want a hint, just look at what Denmark Vesey did when he hit it big. They PURCHASED THEIR FREEDOM! COUNTLESS EXAMPLES of this practice exist! In fact, one of Denmark Vesey's compatriots in the planning of his insurrection, Monday Gell, was hired out and well on his way to purchasing his freedom when he decided to simply fight for it. Mr. Hamilton described Monday as follows in *An Account of the Late Intended Insurrection Among a Portion of the Blacks of the City of Charleston, South Carolina*:

> *Monday Gell* is very well known in this city. He is a most excellent harness-maker, and kept his shop in Meeting street. It would be difficult to name any individual more actively engaged in the plot than himself, or more able to aid Denmark Vesey, from his uncommon sagacity and knowledge. He reads and writes with great and equal facility, and obviously seems to have been the individual who held the pen at all the meetings; at which he wrote more than *one* letter to San Domingo, for succours. His own situation afforded no excuse for the effort in which he was engaged as he enjoyed all the substantial comforts of a freeman; much indulged and trusted by his master, his time and a large proportion of the profits of his labour were at his own disposal.[94]

Monday Gell was a slave with swag. He fought for his rights along with Denmark Vesey and was educated as he "held the pen at all the meetings." He enjoyed freedom as he hired himself out as an excellent harness maker in HIS OWN SHOP on Meeting Street and he made money!

---

[94] Hamilton, 22.

In his 1911 classic *The Negro in Pennsylvania*, Dr. Edward Raymond Turner wrote "sometimes negroes had saved enough to purchase their liberty...frequently one member of a negro family bought freedom for another, the husband often paying for his wife, the father for his children."[95] And Footnote 31 of the same text gives the following accounts:

> 31 In 1779 a negro of Bucks County to secure the freedom of his wife gave his note to be paid by 1783. In 1782, having paid part, he was allowed to take his wife until the next payment. In 1785 she was free. MS. Rec. Pa. Soc. Abol. Sl., I, 27-43. In 1787 negro Samson had purchased his wife and children for ninety-nine pounds. Ibid., I, 67. James Oronogue, who had been hired by his master to the keeper of a tavern, gained by his obliging behavior sixty pounds from the customers within four years' time, and at his master's death was allowed to purchase his freedom for one hundred pounds. He paid besides fifty pounds for his wife. Ibid., I, 69. When Cuff Douglas had been a slave for thirty-seven years his master promised him freedom after four years more. On the master agreeing to take thirty pounds in lieu of this service, Douglas hired himself out, and was free at the end of sixteen months. He then began business as a tailor, and presently was able to buy his wife and children for ninety pounds, besides one son for whom he paid forty-five pounds. Ibid., I, 72. Also ibid., I, 79, 91.[96]

You were not taught anything about these slaves. Some call this revisionist history, but honestly it's just the rest of the story. You KNEW there were other slaves out there: slaves who fought, were educated, had freedom and money, but you did not have the details. Compare the concept of a slave purchasing his freedom from his enslaver with what you were taught about slaves! Imagine the process and semantics of a slave approaching his master, speaking good English because he is educated and saying 'I would like to purchase myself and my family from you. What will it take?' The enslaver doesn't whip him or ridicule him, but he answers him. 'Well, it will take x number of dollars for you and an additional x number of dollars for your family.' Then the slave

---

[95] Dr. Edward Raymond Turner. *The Negro in Pennsylvania, Slavery – Servitude – Freedom, 1639-1861.* Washington, D.C.: American Historical Association, 1911. 61-2.
[96] Turner, 62.

says 'okay', does his work for the enslaver, then hires himself out, saves his money and re-approaches the enslaver and says 'here is the money for me. I will be back for my family.' Goes out and works full time for himself, now that he is free, raises enough money to buy his family's freedom, comes back to the enslaver with a few thousand dollars and says here you go! Picture it Brothers and Sisters. Gain strength from the knowledge of the strength of that brother years ago. Imagine him! In fact, you don't have to imagine him or her and others because their histories exist!

John Berry Meachum was born the slave of one Paul Meachum in Goochland County, Virginia, May 3, 1789. In 1846, John Meachum wrote *An Address to All the Colored Citizens of the United States* where he explains how he purchased his freedom.

> I belonged to a man by the name of Paul Meachum, who moved to North Carolina, and lived there nine years. He then moved to Hardin county [sp], Kentucky, where I still remained a slave with him. He was a good man and I loved him, but could not feel myself satisfied, for he was very old, and looked as if death was drawing near to him. So I proposed to him to hire my time, and he granted it. By working in a saltpetre cave I earned enough to purchase my freedom.
>
> Still I was not satisfied, for I had left my father in old Virginia, and he was a slave. It seemed to me, at times, though I was seven hundred miles from him, that I held conversation with him, for he was near my heart. However this did not stop here, for industry will do a great deal. In a short time I went to Virginia, and bought my father, and paid one hundred pounds for him, Virginia money.[97]

John B. Meachum hired himself out and purchased his freedom and his father's freedom from their respective enslavers! Mr. Meachum wasn't done there. He continued:

> I married a slave in Kentucky, whose master soon took her to St. Louis, in Missouri. I followed her, arriving there in 1815, with three dollars in my pocket. Being a carpenter and cooper I soon obtained business, and purchased my wife and children. Since that period, I have purchased about twenty slaves, most of whom paid back the greatest part of the money, and some paid all. They are all free at this time, and doing well, excepting one, who happened to be a drunkard, and no drunkard can do

---

[97] John Berry Meachum. *An Address to All the Colored Citizens of the United States. Philadelphia, Printed by* King and Baird, 1846. 3.

well. One of the twenty colored friends that I bought is worthy to be taken notice of, to show what industry will do. I paid for him one thousand dollars. He worked and paid back the thousand dollars. He has also bought a lot of ground for which he paid a thousand dollars. He married a slave and bought her, and paid seven hundred dollars for her. He has built a house that cost him six hundred dollars. He is a blacksmith, and has worked for one man ever since he has been in St. Louis.[98]

In St. Louis, Mr. Meachum was known as Reverend John Berry Meachum, founder and Pastor of the First African Baptist Church of St. Louis. An article published in the December 10, 1836 Liberator published in Boston stated First African Baptist had "220 members of whom 200 are slaves" which Mr. Meachum helped to educate. When the authorities caused him problems for teaching slaves within the state of Missouri, Mr. Meachum built a steamboat that included a library on the Mississippi River, which was federal property, to continue his endeavor.[99] And you thought Harriet Tubman was the only slave to free other slaves! Rev. John Berry Meachum was a slave with freedom and money. His picture is available at http://www.firstbaptistchurchstlouis.org/history.

The Reverend William Troy was born March 10, 1827 in Essex County, Virginia to a free Black woman and an enslaved Black man. Since William's mother was free, he was free. William wrote a book titled *Hair-breadth Escapes From Slavery to Freedom* in 1861 where he gave brief biographies of slaves who gained their freedom. His father's story is as follows:

> My father was the son of his master, and, during a portion of his master's life, his domestic servant. His master died, and left him still a slave, to be, with the rest of the property, divided among several lawful children. When the estate was divided, my father was fortunate enough to fall into the hands of one of the daughters, named Jane. Jane had taken a liking to my father. My father then commenced making boots and shoes, and became a first-class workman. He afterwards hired himself out through a medium which the law required. He was then living upon a plantation called Hunter's Hill, He afterwards

---

[98] Meachum, 4-5.
[99] "Capacity of Negroes To Take Care of Themselves," *The Liberator*, December 10, 1836.

moved to a village called Loretto, in the same county. There his business in the shoe trade increased rapidly, and he soon acquired sufficient means to purchase his freedom. He did not, however, purchase his freedom just as soon as he was able to do so; for, had he purchased his freedom, he would have been obliged to leave the State,--the law explicitly saying that it is not permitted to a slave to purchase himself, and remain.

My father, however, soon became tired of that sort of life, and paid the value of himself through the hands of my mother. A bill of sale was passed into my mother's hands, thus making him the property of my mother. She, however, soon gave him papers of manumission.[100]

In *The Negro in Maryland*, Mr. Brackett tells us of a Black woman who bartered for her freedom. This Black woman made a deal with her mistress that in exchange for leaving to live with her husband in another territory, the Black woman will raise the mistress' two young children. The deal went down as planned and the slave woman had four kids after the 1831 deal. When those children were of age, they petitioned for and received their freedom formally, but thanks to the love and affection of their mother, they were informally free since birth.[101] Only God knows how this Black woman pulled off such a deal, as one would have to assume she would have been forced to raise the mistress' children as a slave any way. Never doubt the ingenuity of the Black woman! On July 26, 1824 a free Black woman named Fanny Teackle manumitted her man Willis in Accomack County, Virginia. The manumission papers read:

Know all men by these presents that I Fanny Teackle Black woman have Manumitted set free & forever discharged from Slavery my Negro man Willis whom I purchased of William M. Scarborough hereby relinquishing all claims right title & interest which I have in the said Willis forever
In Testimony whereof I have hereunto set my hand and affixed my seal this 26th day of July 1824[102]

---

[100] Rev. William Troy. *Hair-breadth Escapes from Slavery to Freedom.* Manchester, England: 1861. 2-3.
[101] Brackett, 173.
[102] Accomack County District Court and Superior Court Miscellaneous Papers 1789 – 1850, Manumission Papers, July 26, 1824. Online at http://easternshoreheritage.com.

Mr. Samuel R. Lowery was born in Nashville, Tennessee. Dr. Simmons highlighted Mr. Lowery's life in *Men of Mark* and states "his mother was a free woman, a Cherokee Indian, and his father a slave, living twelve miles from the said city, and was purchased by his wife; God bless the woman."[103] Just to be clear, Samuel Lowery's FREE Cherokee mother purchased the freedom of her husband who was the enslaved Black father of Samuel. Ruth and Peter Lowery did a fantastic job rearing Samuel as he grew up to be a successful silk culturalist, lawyer, editor and principal of an industrial institute.[104] The February 1880 New York Times newspaper had this to say about Mr. Lowery:

> WASHINGTON, Feb. 2. - Samuel R. Lowery, colored, President of an industrial academy in Huntsville, Ala., was admitted to practice before the United States Supreme Court to-day, on motion of Mrs. Belva A. Lockwood, attorney, of this city. Mr. Lowery was admitted to practice in the Connty [sp] Court of Davidson County Tenn., in 1870; in the Court of Common Pleas, in the same place, a few days later, and two months afterward in the Court of Appeals of Tennessee, at Nashville. In April, 1876, he was admitted to practice in the United States Circuit Court of the Northern District of Alabama. He was formerly a student at Howard University. Mr. Lowery is the fifth colored lawyer admitted to practice in the United States Supreme Court The first was J.S. Rock, of Boston; another is J.H. Cook, of this city, and another, John M. Langston, formerly professor in Howard University and now Minister to Hayti.[105]

Now, before reading this article, how many of you would have believed a Black man, who was never a slave, was admitted to practice law before the Supreme Court in 1880? Now, how many of you would have believed there were four other Black men who practiced in the Supreme Court before him? Not many at all! But hopefully the names, stories and documented references of these men will convince you otherwise. Just in case they don't, here is a picture of Mr. Samuel R. Lowery:

---

[103] Simmons, 144.
[104] Simmons, 144-8.
[105] "A Colored Lawyer's Mission. Samuel R. Lowery Admitted to Practice In The United States Supreme Court-His Plan For Educating His People," *New York Times*, February 3, 1880.

Figure 36 Samuel R. Lowery was born free in Nashville, TN. His free mother purchased the freedom of his slave father.

Bartlett Taylor was born a slave February 14, 1815 in Henderson County, Kentucky. He hired himself out as a butcher in Louisville, Kentucky and made considerable money. He was hired to one of Louisville's largest beef merchants, Mr. Clisindoff, and cleared nearly $300 per year. He knew the sale of his person was pending so Mr. Taylor worked extra hard and saved $1,800 to purchase himself from his enslaver. Unfortunately, he was scammed out of his money a little before he was scheduled to hit the auction block. On September 20, 1840 Mr. Taylor went up for sale in front of La Grange Court House. He participated in the bidding and was his own highest bidder at $2,000. After the sale concluded, Mr. Taylor told the manager of the sale, Mr. Brent, that he had no money to pay at the moment but would earn the money as soon as possible. God was with Mr. Taylor that day because Mr. Brent extended him his freedom papers on credit! Mr. Taylor paid the $2,000 debt off by the end of the year. He was a slave with freedom and money![106]

Randall Bartholomew Vandavall (also spelled Vandervall) was born a slave in 1832 at Neeley's Bend on the Cumberland River near Nashville, Tennessee. Randall's

---

[106] Simmons, 626-30.

initial enslaver was Major Hall who also enslaved Randall's mother Sylvonia. Randall's father was a slave named Lewis who drove a coach for his enslaver named Foster. Lewis was only allowed to visit Sylvonia once a year, yet they were able to have 11 children together including Randall. Major Hall's death kicked off Randall's expedition from enslaver to enslaver, the first move being the most painful as he was separated from his mother but also very rewarding as he was allowed to attend school and was assisted with his 'letters' by White children of the house. Randall had a few stints with some very cruel enslavers, much like those you learned about in school, and eventually was purchased by a Mr. Vandavall whom he is named after.

When he was 15, Randall wanted to increase his learning so he worked a deal where he hired himself out as a rail splitter in order to pay for school. His enslaver's son, John Vandavall, also assisted young Randall with his education. Randall eventually married Miss Martha Nicholson, still as a slave. About that time he hired his time for $200 a year so he could go to Nashville and work. He also hired his wife's time from her enslaver so she could go with him. At the time Randall was hiring his own time, he was sold to another enslaver named Mr. Barter who did not impede Randall. While in Nashville, Randall heard Mr. Barter was planning to sell him again, so Mr. Randall Vandavall went home to have a man-to-man talk with Mr. Barter. Dr. Simmons documented that conversation as follows:

> ...Mr. Barter said it was not so, but his wife said it was. After some conversation, he told them he could not believe that they could sell him, as they had promised not to do so. Mr. Vandervall said to him, "God is just, and every man shall have to give an account of himself to God. Now, Mr. Barter, how would you like it to be treated as you have treated me?" "I should not like it," said he. He threw the blame on his wife, and said she would not rest until it was done. He then asked Mr. Barter what he was to do, and then Mr. Barter swore that he would not sign the papers.
> Vandervall then asked them to let him keep on paying for his time as he had started to do, and further asked if he had

ever been untrue to them, or ever gave them any trouble. They answered "No." He then asked why he wanted to sell him from his wife. To this they made no reply. Mr. Barter then said that he was willing that Vandervall should have a chance to buy himself, if he could do so. This was agreed upon, and the price fixed at $1800, $500 cash.[107]

At the end of the day, Mr. Barter ended up selling Mr. Vandavall just as Mrs. Barter wished. Randall's wife was also sold by her enslaver. Thankfully the same man, Mr. Nelson Nicholson, had enough kindness in his heart to purchase both Randall Vandavall and his wife and he did so primarily to keep them together.

Both Vandavall's hired their time out from their new enslaver, Mr. Nicholson, so they could continue to live together in Nashville. They were never able to flat out purchase their freedom, but did hire their time until freed by the war. After he was freed, Mr. Randall Vandavall became the Rev. Dr. Randall Vandavall! He founded Vandavall's Baptist Church, later renamed First Baptist Church of East Nashville and was a prominent educator of Black people, so much so that Roger Williams University conferred him an honorary Doctorate of Divinity degree in 1886. One of his sons earned a medical degree from Central Tennessee College and three of his other children were educated at Roger Williams University.[108] Here is Rev. Dr. Randall Bartholomew Vandavall:

---

[107] Simmons, 575-6. Most other sources used the last name spelling as Vandavall, but Mr. Simmons used Vandervall.
[108] Simmons, 572-8.

Figure 37 The resilient Rev. Randall B. Vandavall (a.k.a. Vandervall). A slave with swag.

Edmond Kelley was born a slave in Tennessee sometime in 1817. As a child he served as a waiter to his enslaver who happened to be the headmaster at a school. Edmond was in contact with the students at the school and was able to convince them to teach him in exchange for sweets Edmond stole from his enslaver.[109] As an adult slave, Edmond married a slave from another homestead, Miss Paralee Walker, on Sept. 15, 1839 and was ordained to preach on May 19, 1842. (Yes, as a slave). Around 1843, Edmond became Pastor of the First Baptist Church of Columbia, Tennessee by paying his enslaver, who was now one Nancy White, $10 per month for his time. So, not only did Edmond hire himself out, but this pious soul hired himself out to the Church to do God's work. In 1846, Nancy White's estate ran into financial trouble and she was in jeopardy of losing her assets which included Edmond. Instead of losing him, she urged him to go away and preach the word of God,

---

[109] Simmons, 291.

so on November 15, 1846, she had her lawyer draw up the following pass:

> State of Tennessee, Robertson County. Know all men by these presents, that I, Hugh Robertson, of the County and State aforesaid, by virtue of a power of Attorney to me executed on the 15th day of November, 1846, by Nancy White, of the County of Maury, and State aforesaid, do hereby authorize and permit a mulatto boy, Edmond Kelley, a Baptist preacher, to go to any State in the United States of America, and to preach, and to remain when and where he pleases until he is called for by the owner, or myself as her Attorney in fact. This the 4th day of January, 1847.
>
> NANCY WHITE. By her Attorney, HUGH ROBERTSON.[110]

Edmond's pass was bitter sweet as he got to roam the country as a free man, but his wife and children had different enslavers and weren't given their freedom. With this pass, Edmond travelled the country preaching the word of God but longed for the freedom of his wife and four children. He ultimately ended up the Pastor of the Second Street Baptist Church in New Bedford, Massachusetts which is now known as Myrtle Baptist Church. You can read the history of Myrtle Baptist Church (which mentions Edmond Kelly) at http://www.myrtlebaptist.org/welcome/about-myrtle/our-history/myrtle -history).

Rev. Edmond Kelley had remained in contact with his wife, Paralee Walker, and now started exchanging letters with his wife's enslaver James Walker WHO ALSO HAPPENED TO BE HIS WIFE'S FATHER! On February 24, 1850 James Walker replied to Edmond Kelley's question: if James would sell Kelley's wife and four children, Paralee, Dolly Ophelia, Robert Edmond, William Dempsey, and Alfred to Kelley and at what price? Here is James Walker's response:

> Columbia, *Feb. 24,* 1850.
> REV. EDMOND KELLEY,--SIR: Yours of the 12th inst. addressed to my wife, has been handed to me. You respectfully ask for information that I am willing to give you. In

---

[110] Edmond Kelley. *A Family Redeemed from Bondage; Being Rev. Edmond Kelley, (the Author,) His Wife, and Four Children.* New Bedford, MA: Edmond Kelley Publisher, 1851. 7. Also available online as part of the University of North Carolina digitization project at http://docsouth.unc.edu/neh/kelley/kelley.html.

the first place, if they were offered for sale here at the present prices of such servants, they would command in each $2,800. No price, however, could be offered by any one that would induce me to permit them to be the slaves or servants of any but my own family. To part with them, with certain knowledge that they were to be free, and their condition bettered, is a matter I might take into consideration. But it is useless to do so until you inform me you can command $2,800, to be applied to that object.

Dolly, the mother of your wife, was my nurse, took the tenderest care of me when I was an orphan child. The attachment which this has produced on my part, and on the part of my wife and children to her and her children and their children, and their treatment, is altogether different from what is ordinarily termed *slavery*. Although they occupy the position of servants to me and my family, they in reality, in the tie of affection and regard for their comfort and happiness which exists, are not *slaves* at all. They, *if they are colored,* stand next in my affections to my own wife and children and children's children. The affection I believe to be mutual. Now, if you could command the means to pay for and emancipate them, could you provide for and place them in a happier and more comfortable condition than they now are, and have every guarantee of remaining? This is the question to be considered and satisfactorily answered before I will take the matter into consideration. I much doubt your ability to make the change you desire beneficial to them, if I were even voluntarily to emancipate them. This I shall not do, for the simple reason that I believe doing so would not benefit them, if there were no other reason. But I have other reasons. My family are accustomed to and must have servants. Servants to whom they are attached, and who are truly attached to them, are invaluable. Servants who are raised up in a family, perfectly honest and upright, attached to those who are their owners and protectors, are a necessary part of a family, not conveniently dispensed with, not calculated to promote the happiness and welfare of either owner or servants, unless under the existence of unusual circumstances.

I never blamed you for exercising the natural right of securing your freedom if you could. This was your natural right, and in exercising it you committed no offence against your God, whose approbation alone is to be looked to. But in doing this, have you made yourself happier and in better circumstances than you would have been here? Perhaps you have, but the effect may be different if you could accomplish what you wish in relation to your wife and children. Their situation may be, and probably is, entirely different from what yours was. They are in no danger of being sold, uncertain to whom.

If you have the means of raising $2,800 for the emancipation of your wife and children, and can satisfy me that you have the further ability of providing a comfortable support for them, and will inform me of the fact, I will take the matter into consideration. If you cannot do this, and have the means to furnish me with to purchase whatever claim may be upon your labor and services here, and have *you emancipated,* my attachment to your wife and children would make me take much trouble to accomplish any wish you may have to live here a free man with your wife and children *nominally slaves.*

Yours, &c.,
JAMES WALKER.[111]

The many facets and dynamics of these relationships and this letter are absolutely intriguing! Here you have Edmond Kelley, a slave who has a pass to roam the country freely preaching the word of God asking to purchase his wife and children from an enslaver who is the father of his wife and grandfather to his children! Doesn't the dual role of James as enslaver and father ring true in the letter? As enslaver, James is saying I will sell them to you if you guarantee me $2,800 for all of them, despite the fact I can get $2,800 for each of them. But as a father he's saying you can have my daughter and grandchildren only if you can provide for them just as well or better than I have! Who would have thought that was even possible? A slave roaming the country, who is a Pastor of a church, knows how to read and write, AND writing a letter to an enslaver requesting to buy his slaves! And at the end of the day, James Walker did in fact agree to sell Paralee, Dolly Ophelia, Robert Edmond, William Dempsey, and Alfred Kelley to their husband/father Edmond Kelley for $2,800 plus $365 transportation costs. On May 30, 1851 Edmond Kelley reunited with his wife and children in New Bedford, Massachusetts. Later that year, Edmond Kelly published a book titled *A Family Redeemed from Bondage; Being Rev. Edmond Kelley, (the Author,) His Wife, and Four Children* that detailed the whole experience.[112] Slaves had freedom and money people. Slaves had FREEDOM AND MONEY. SLAVES HAD FREEDOM AND MONEY!

---

[111] Kelley, 9-10.
[112] See *A Family Redeemed from Bondage* for other intimate details of Kelley's journey.

6 Slaves with Swag

When a person, any person enslaved or otherwise, is willing to fight, is educated, has freedom and money, they will most likely have a swagger about them. All the cold, hard FACTS presented to you up to this point thoroughly prove that slaves (ex-slaves) were fighters, were educated, and had freedom as well as money. They also had swag! Let's examine a few prime examples.

Dr. Rev. Isaac M. Burgan

Remember the little slave boy mentioned at the beginning of this book named Isaac Burgan? You know, the one who whacked the overseer on the back of the head as the overseer whipped his mother? Well, in addition to being a fighter, Isaac Burgan was educated, had freedom, money and possessed power. When Isaac grew a little older, Dr. Simmons documented, "he hired out for a small sum per month, most of which was required to purchase winter clothing and shoes for his mother."[113] About the time the war ended and all the slaves were freed, Isaac ended up in Tennessee where he worked hard on the railroad. He was able to save several hundred dollars and used it to fund about a year's worth of education at Bowling Green, Kentucky. At the end of that year, he worked different jobs in several cities in the pursuit of raising additional funds for school as well as food, clothing and shelter.

---

[113] Simmons, 1087.

Slaves With Swag

In Evansville in October 1870, he attended public school taught by the Dr. Rev. J. M. Townsend while working for white families for room and board. Here is a picture of Dr. Rev. Townsend:

Figure 38 Preeminent Black teacher Dr. Rev. J. M. Townsend who guided Isaac M. Burgan. While Mr. Burgan was a slave with swag, the Dr. Rev. Townsend was a free Black man (Category 3) with swag. He was born in 1841.

Understandably, young Burgan got tired of serving White families, even though some of them treated him fairly, so he moved to Terre Haute where he attended the State Normal School at Terre Haute and stayed in a boarding house. He was an outstanding student, particularly "standing preeminent in mathematics and philosophy"[114] while working as a cook and housekeeper at the post office. Dr. Simmons summarized Mr. Burgan's daily routines as follows:

> Work was soon secured which yielded ten dollars per month; but this was a dear income, for it had to be earned during the cold winters of 1873 and 1874, between five and seven o'clock in the morning. Very often this untiring student of the Normal school had to plunge into the darkness of the morning amid snow, rain and sleet, to get the post office cleaned and warmed by seven o'clock. The rush did not stop here, for hurry must be made to the baker's for a loaf of bread, and to the butcher's for his meat, and go home, make his fire, prepare his breakfast, and be at school by 8:45. But he braved it till school closed in the spring.[115]

The boarding house was seven blocks from the post office.

---

[114] Simmons, 1088.
[115] Simmons, 1089.

After five terms at the Terre Haute Normal School, Isaac ran out of money and energy. He dropped out of school temporarily and went to Lost Creek to begin teaching; after all he did have five terms of education. He taught at Lost Creek until September 1878 where he entered Wilberforce University to study divinity. He was such a good student and able man of God, Wilberforce granted him a scholarship of $60.00 per year. Now able to focus on his studies full-time, the Rev. Isaac Burgan graduated Wilberforce as VALEDICTORIAN and was hired as President of Paul Quinn College in Waco, Texas! Paul Quinn is a HBCU and it is still in existence today. Rev. Isaac Burgan served as President of Paul Quinn from 1883 to 1891 then again from 1911 to 1914.[116] In between serving as President of Paul Quinn, Rev. Burgan preached the word of God in Oakland, California; Richmond, Indiana; and Vincennes, Indiana. He also received a Doctor of Divinity degree from Philander Smith College which is still in existence in Little Rock, Arkansas. Again, here is the esteemed, hard-working, mother-protecting Dr. Rev. Isaac M. Burgan:

Figure 39 Dr. Rev. Isaac M. Burgan.

He was a slave with swag.

---

[116] Paul Quinn College website, www.pqc.edu, November 2011.

John Mitchell Jr.

John Mitchell Jr. was born July 11, 1863 in Henrico County, Virginia. His father was a coachman and his mother was a seamstress. Both of his parents were slaves, which made John Jr. a slave even if only for a couple years. After they received their freedom, John's mother proceeded to teach him how to read. Dr. Simmons puts it as "His mother taught him his a, b, c's, a-b ab's and e-b eb's and the other monosyllabic beginnings, in that old antiquated method..."[117] John continued to be instructed by his mother and "felt the full force of her hand on his young face to enable him to have a better appreciation of his lessons"[118] until he entered a grade school lead by Rev. Anthony Binga, Jr. and the Richmond Normal High School in 1877.

Figure 40 Another one of those little known of 1800's Black educators, Rev. Anthony Binga Jr.

While still in school, young John was a newsboy (which would have great influence on his adult life) and also a carriage boy for his parents' former enslaver James Lyons. Mr. Lyons was a wealthy lawyer who took offense to young John being educated, but since they were free, John continued his formal learning as his mother wished. But that

---

[117] Simmons, 315.
[118] Simmons, 315.

didn't stop Mr. Lyons from trying to keep young John in an inferior position by responding negatively whenever a Black person would come to his door. John had respect for his people, so whenever he would answer Mr. Lyons' door and a Black man was on the other side of it, young John as the carriage boy would alert Mr. Lyons that "a colored gentlemen wished to see him." Mr. Lyons with contempt in his heart would aptly retort there are no colored gentlemen.[119]

These encounters affected John Mitchell Jr., but not in the way Mr. Lyons' intended. It fueled young John to become a 'race man'. After finishing school and gaining some notoriety as a map drafter and orator, young John became the Richmond correspondent of the New York Freeman and shortly after that he became editor of the Richmond Planet which was a weekly newspaper published in Richmond, Virginia. Mr. Mitchell was FEARLESS with his content in the Richmond Planet, particularly content that addressed lynching and the unjust prosecution of Black people. Dr. Simmons summarizes below:

> The lynching of Richard Walker, in Charlotte county [sp], demonstrated Mr. Mitchell's courage again. This colored man was lynched by a mob of white men at Smithville, about eighty-six miles from Richmond, Virginia. Mr. Mitchell condemned the affair and declared that his murderers should be dangled from a rope's end. This occurred in May, 1886. The editorial appeared on a Saturday, and on the following Monday he [John Mitchell Jr.] received a letter containing a piece of hemp, abusing him and declaring they would hang him, should he put his foot in the county. Mr. Mitchell replied that he would visit the county, adding: "There are no terrors, Cassius, in your threats, for I am armed so strong in honesty that they pass me by like the idle winds, which I respect not."
> Later on he armed himself with a brace of Smith & Wesson revolvers, went to the scene of the murder, which was five miles from any railroad station, and was locked in the jail for the purpose of inspecting the place where Walker had been found, and then returned to Richmond and published an account of his trip.[120]

[119] Simmons, 315.
[120] Simmons, 319-20.

Slaves With Swag

The Richmond Planet was full of anti-lynching propaganda. The July 2, 1898 edition exclaimed:

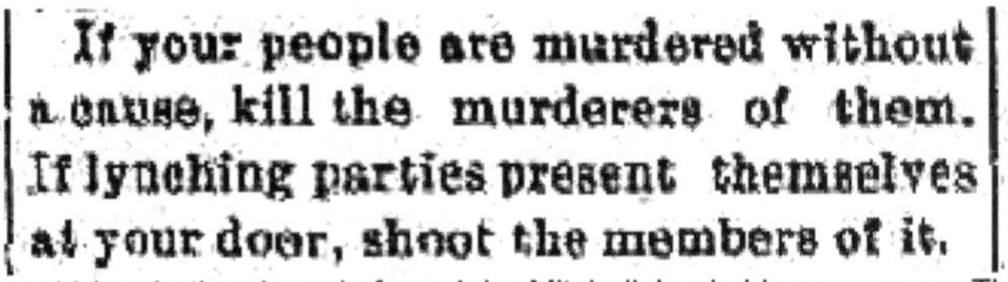

> If your people are murdered without a cause, kill the murderers of them. If lynching parties present themselves at your door, shoot the members of it.

Figure 41 Inspirational words from John Mitchell Jr. via his newspaper, The Richmond Planet.[121]

Many issues of the papers kept a running total of lynchings in the U.S., both Black and White, and spoke vehemently against them. The Richmond Planet was a staunch supporter of Black businesses in the Richmond area and ran countless ads supporting the same. Mr. Mitchell made sure his paper supported his culture and placed it in a positive light. You should be aware of his existence, efforts, opinions, theories and philosophies. The July 12, 1890 edition of the Richmond Planet addressed colored voting as follows:

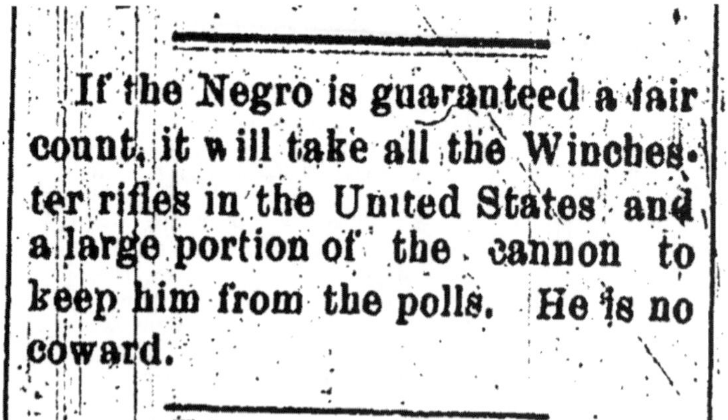

> If the Negro is guaranteed a fair count, it will take all the Winchester rifles in the United States and a large portion of the cannon to keep him from the polls. He is no coward.

Figure 42 Inspirational words from John Mitchell Jr. via his newspaper, The Richmond Planet.[122]

In that same edition, he provided encouragement for other ex-slaves as follows:

---

[121] Richmond Planet, July 2, 1898. 4.
[122] Richmond Planet, July 12, 1890. 2.

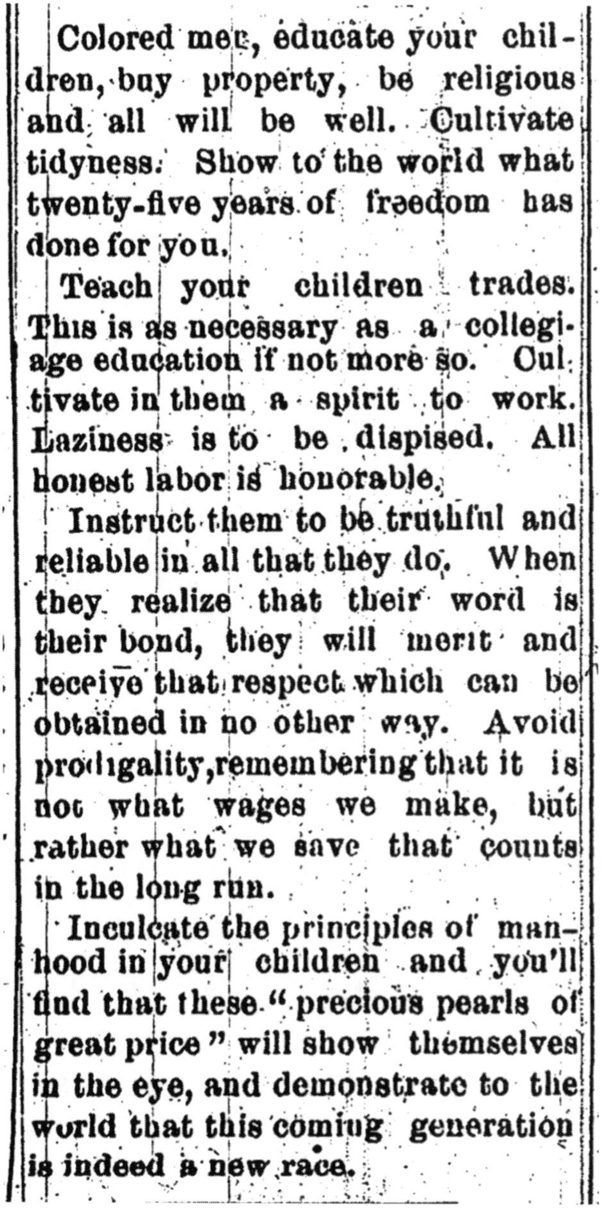

Colored men, educate your children, buy property, be religious and, all will be well. Cultivate tidyness. Show to the world what twenty-five years of freedom has done for you.

Teach your children trades. This is as necessary as a collegiage education if not more so. Cultivate in them a spirit to work. Laziness is to be dispised. All honest labor is honorable.

Instruct them to be truthful and reliable in all that they do. When they realize that their word is their bond, they will merit and receive that respect which can be obtained in no other way. Avoid prodigality, remembering that it is not what wages we make, but rather what we save that counts in the long run.

Inculcate the principles of manhood in your children and you'll find that these "precious pearls of great price" will show themselves in the eye, and demonstrate to the world that this coming generation is indeed a new race.

Figure 43 Inspirational words from John Mitchell Jr. via his newspaper, The Richmond Planet.[123]

[123] Richmond Planet, July 12, 1890. 2.

Slaves With Swag

The July 27, 1889 edition provided the following instruction for Black men:

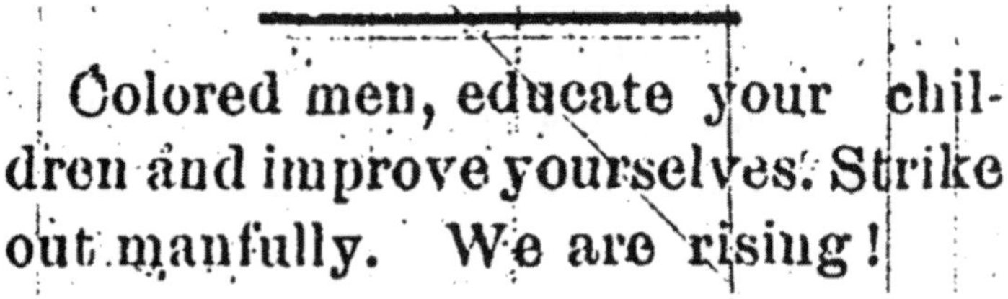

Colored men, educate your children and improve yourselves. Strike out manfully. We are rising!

Figure 44 Inspirational words from John Mitchell Jr. via his newspaper, The Richmond Planet.[124]

And...

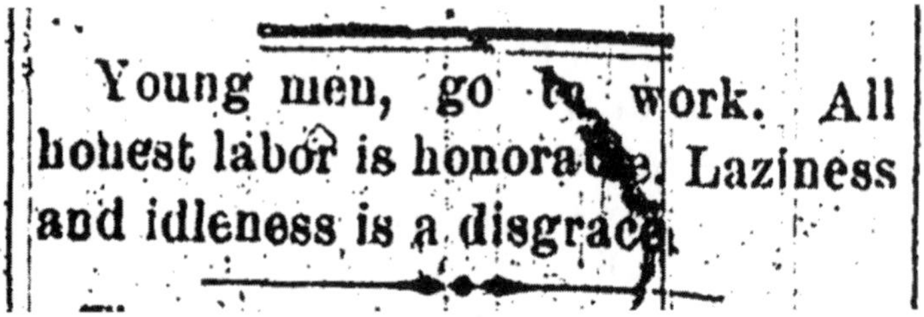

Young men, go to work. All honest labor is honorable. Laziness and idleness is a disgrace.

Figure 45 Inspirational words from John Mitchell Jr. via his newspaper, The Richmond Planet.[125]

From 1884 to his death in 1929, John Mitchell Jr. honorably stood at the helm of the Richmond Planet which was located at 814 East Broad Street in the city of Richmond.

Figure 46 Logo of The Richmond Planet.[126]

The clips offered here do not give justice to his massive contribution toward the protection and advancement of post-slavery Black folks, but the Virginia library has created an online exhibit in his honor where much more information is available.

---

[124] Richmond Planet, July 27, 1889. 2.
[125] Richmond Planet, July 27, 1889. 2.
[126] Richmond Planet, Jan. 18, 1902. 1.

In addition to running the Richmond Planet, Mr. Mitchell was elected to local political offices, unsuccessfully ran for Governor of Virginia and founded the Mechanics Savings Bank! The bank had moderate success but was only able to succeed a few years due to political retaliation against Mr. Mitchell for all his years of fighting the system. Here is a picture of the outside of the Mechanics Savings Bank which was located at 3rd and Clay Streets, Richmond, Virginia:

Figure 47 You can see a photograph of the bank in the January 1917 Crisis Magazine. If you're in Richmond, the original building is still standing on the corner of 3rd and Clay Streets.[127]

And here is a picture of the prestigious John Mitchell Jr. standing in front of his bank's massive vault:

Figure 48 The article states that Mr. Mitchell was 5' 10" tall to give potential customers an idea of the massiveness of the vault door which would secure their funds. Photo from the November 5, 1910 Richmond Planet.[128]

---

[127] Richmond Planet, Oct. 2, 1909.1.
[128] Richmond Planet, Nov. 5, 1910. 8.

Slaves With Swag

He was a slave with swag!

Figure 49 Mr. John Mitchell Jr., a slave with swag.[129]

Robert Harlan

Robert Harlan was born a slave in Mecklenburg County, Virginia on December 12, 1816. His father was White and his mother was three parts White and one part Black.

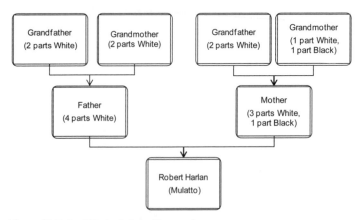

Figure 50 Robert Harlan's hereditary make-up.

Since children assumed the status of their mother, it is safe to assume Robert's mixed maternal grandmother was a slave. That's not to say any of Robert's other grandparents could not have been slaves, because there were plenty of White

---

[129] Richmond Planet, June 16, 1909. 1.

slaves in early America (they were called servants), but that is the subject of a different book. Robert was brought to Kentucky from Virginia when he was eight years-old, where he was purchased by future Congressman and member of the Kentucky House of Representatives James Harlan. Young Robert received exceptional favoritism from his enslaver, more so than any of his other slaves. In fact, Robert Harlan was educated by James' own sons![130]

Like many other slaves, Robert Harlan hired himself out and was the owner/operator of his businesses (remember Monday Gell). Robert had a barbershop in Harrodsburg, Kentucky and a grocery store in Lexington, Kentucky, and he operated both while still a slave. When the California gold rush hit in the late 1840's, Robert WENT TO CALIFORNIA TO PROSPECT (I.E. DIG FOR GOLD) WHILE HE WAS STILL A SLAVE! And guess what? Like Denmark Vesey before him, Robert Harlan hit it big! Dr. Simmons noted that Robert "amassed a fortune of forty-five thousand dollars in gold, which he brought back and invested in Cincinnati, Ohio."[131] And again, like many slaves before him, Robert took $500 of his earnings and purchased his freedom from James Harlan! In Cincinnati, Robert built two fine homes, opened a first class daguerreotype photography studio, and became trustee of Colored Schools and the Colored Orphan Asylum.

In search of a new environment for his family, Robert moved to England in 1858 and stayed there for ten years. The $45,000 he won (which equates to almost $1,000,000 in today's currency) afforded him that opportunity. When he returned, the former slave Robert Harlan was offered foreign consulships and other positions of power by government

---

[130] One of James Harlan's sons was associate Supreme Court Justice John Marshall Harlan. While John Marshall was too young to have taught Robert, some may speculate that Robert's presence affected Justice Harlan's voting on the Supreme Court particularly since he was the only dissenting voice in Plessy v. Ferguson. The dissent he wrote spoke to the equality of the races and the universal application of the U.S. Constitution to all.

[131] Simmons, 613-4.

officials, including President Rutherford B. Hayes and President Chester A. Arthur. Some he accepted (for example the Special Agent of the Treasury Department appointment by Chester A. Arthur and the Special Agent At Large of the Post Office Department under General Grant's administration) and some he did not.[132] He successfully raised and led a colored battalion of troops which earned him the title of Colonel as verified on page 8 of the October 20, 1870 Cincinnati Commercial Tribune:

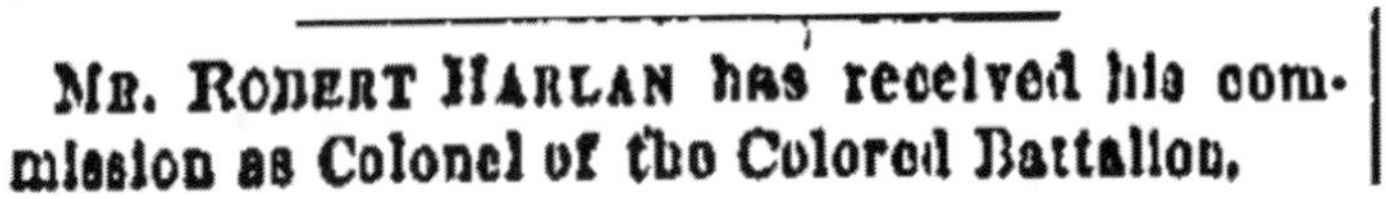

Mr. Robert Harlan has received his commission as Colonel of the Colored Battalion.

Figure 51 American newspaper article documenting the achievement of an ex-slave.[133]

Fourteen years later, the same paper presented a bio of Colonel Robert Harlan, including an etching of him that gave details of his heritage, his life and accomplishments.[134] Regardless of booming successes, Mr. Robert Harlan was consistent in the defense of his Black heritage as demonstrated in the front page article of the February 5, 1887 Cleveland Gazette:

---

[132] Simmons, 613-6.
[133] Cincinnati Commercial Tribune, Oct. 20, 1870. 8.
[134] Cincinnati Commercial Tribune, June 8, 1884. 15. This article also included bios of other slaves with swag such as Blanche K. Bruce, John R. Lynch who was elected and re-elected to the MS state Legislature, and Mr. Robert Heberton Terrell a former slave who graduated from Harvard that year. Mr. Terrell, soon to be known as Judge Terrell, also delivered the student commencement address titled 'The Negro Race in America Since Emancipation.'

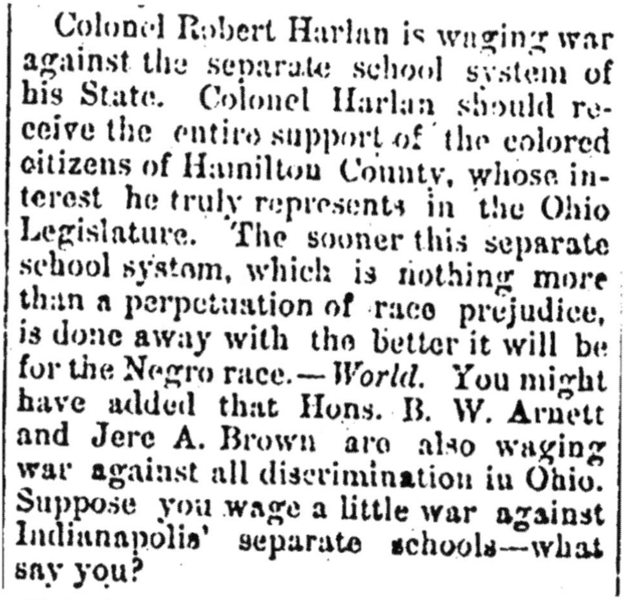

Colonel Robert Harlan is waging war against the separate school system of his State. Colonel Harlan should receive the entire support of the colored citizens of Hamilton County, whose interest he truly represents in the Ohio Legislature. The sooner this separate school system, which is nothing more than a perpetuation of race prejudice, is done away with the better it will be for the Negro race. — *World*. You might have added that Hons. B. W. Arnett and Jere A. Brown are also waging war against all discrimination in Ohio. Suppose you wage a little war against Indianapolis' separate schools—what say you?

Figure 52 American newspaper article documenting the achievement of an ex-slave.[135]

In case you can't read between the lines, this former slave, turned barber, turned business owner, turned gold prospector, turned foreign national, turned photographer, turned trustee, turned Post Office agent, appointed Treasury Department agent, commissioned Colonel had been ELECTED TO THE OHIO STATE LEGISLATURE! He was a slave with swag.

COLONEL ROBERT HARLAN

Figure 53 Colonel Robert Harlan as depicted in the June 8, 1884 Cincinnati Commercial Tribune article.[136]

---

[135] "Some Race Doings," Cleveland Gazette, Feb. 5, 1887. 1.
[136] Cincinnati Commercial Tribune, June 8, 1884. 15.

Figure 54 Here is the "3 part White, 1 part Black" slave with swag, Colonel Robert Harlan as depicted in *Men of Mark*. One drop of Black blood (or in his case 1 part), made him Black, despite his obvious Caucasian features.

Robert Smalls

Robert Smalls was born a slave in Beaufort, South Carolina in the year 1839. Like many of the other slaves mentioned in this book, Robert was not a cotton picking field hand as you have been led to believe all slaves were. Robert was a slave during the Civil War and consequently spent time on Confederate war ships serving his enslavers, which gave him the perfect experience for his magnificent feat.

In 1862 Robert was acting as pilot on the Confederate steamship named the Planter. On May 12 of that year, the ship docked at Charleston, South Carolina after transporting guns for two weeks straight. Since the ship docked at its home port, all of the Planter's Confederate crew went on shore, leaving the slaves behind to tend the ship. Little did they know 23 year-old Robert had already derived a plan to commandeer the Planter and deliver it to Union forces and the Confederate crew's absence from the ship afforded Mr. Smalls his opportunity! He quickly consulted with the eight other slave crew members and he found those Brothers ready to ride and/or die for their freedom. They figured their intimate knowledge of how to run the ship and familiarity with the South Carolina waterways, particularly Robert who served as the pilot, increased their odds of success. So at about 2 am on the 13th of May these courageous men quietly fired up the Planter and off they went.

At the time Robert was a devoted husband and father of two children, despite his slave status, and he wasn't about to leave his wife and children in the thralls of slavery while he sailed to Union land. So he and the Brothers made a stop on their way out at the North Atlantic Wharf where they picked up Robert's wife, two children, as well as four other slave women and one more slave child, most likely the families of the other crew members. Since Robert was a veteran on the South Carolina waterways, he easily made his way through the guarded Confederate ports. Now, how did a Confederate warship, full of slaves, in South Carolina make it through armed Confederate soldier guards at numerous ports? Without any White sailors on board, might you ask? Understand, slaves were not the ignorant, half-wits your education has left you to believe. Robert had planned this mission out with intricate detail who knows how long before its actual execution. He had been through those guarded ports countless times as the slave pilot of the Planter. He knew the secret signals to blow at each port to gain permission to pass and noted the Captain's dress and physical mannerisms so he could mimic them. He even went as far as to don the Captain's trademark big straw hat and fold his arms across his chest just like the Confederate Captain to fool the guards who were at a disadvantage due to the distance between land and the ship and the time of night (remember, they left at 2 am). Once Robert, his crew and his passengers cleared the last Confederate port, he removed the Confederate flag, raised the white flag of truce and delivered the Planter, all its valuable ammunition and his now free passengers to the Union!

Once the news that a slave had commandeered a Confederate ship and delivered it to the Federal Fleet hit the street, Robert's story went viral and he became an overnight sensation as well as a national hero. Not long after the takeover, rumor began to spread that Robert had asked permission to relocate to Central America. To quell the rumor, Robert wrote the following letter which was posted in scores of newspapers up and down the East Coast. This one is from the front page of the September 13, 1862, Vermont Journal:

A PATRIOTIC NEGRO.—Some of our friends, who cannot fight nor encourage others to defend the country, unless the President adopts their particular policy, will do well to consider the example of Robert Smalls, the gallant negro pilot, who brought the rebel steamer Planter out of Charleston, and delivered her to our navy. He sends this letter to the Washington Republican:

Mr. Editor;

In your paper of yesterday it is stated that an application had been made by me to Senator Pomeroy for a passage to Central America. I wish it understood that I have made no such application; but, at the same time, I would express my cordial approval of every kind and wise effort for the liberation and elevation of my oppressed race. After waiting apparently in vain, for many years for our deliverance, a party consisting of nine men, myself included, of the City of Charleston, conferred freedom on ourselves, five women and three children ; and to the Government of the United States we gave the Planter, a gunboat, which cost nearly $30,000, together with six large guns from a 24-pounder howitzer to a 100-pound Parrott rifle. We are all now in the service of the Navy, under, the command of our true friend, Rear Admiral Dupont; where we wish to serve till the rebellion and slavery are crushed out forever.

Very respectfully,
ROBERT SMALLS.

Figure 55 American newspaper documentation of a slave with swag.[137]

Bear witness to the bravery and intelligence of this former slave! You would think his delivery of a Confederate ship with guns and ammunition would be enough for him to live out the rest of his days in absolute glory, but no, he pledged to fight on until 'the rebellion and slavery' were 'crushed out forever!' That's a man! What bravery! And fight on is exactly what Robert Smalls did. Dr. Simmons documented the rest of Captain Smalls' battles by quoting a record of the House of Representatives, Forty-seventh Congress as follows:

Captain Smalls was soon afterwards ordered to Edisto to join the gunboat *Crusader,* Captain Rhind. He then proceeded in the *Crusader,* piloting her and followed by the *Planter* to Simmons' Bluff, on Wadmalaw Sound, where a sharp battle was fought between these boats and a Confederate light battery and some infantry. The Confederates were driven out of their works, and the troops on the *Planter* landed and captured all the tents and provisions of the enemy. This occurred some time in June, 1862.

Captain Smalls continued to act as pilot on board the *Planter* and the *Crusades,* and as blockading pilot between Charleston and Beaufort. He made repeated trips up and along the rivers near the coast, pointing out and removing the

---

[137] Vermont Journal, Sep. 13, 1862. 1.

torpedoes which he himself had assisted in sinking and putting in position. During these trips he was present in several fights at Adams' Rum on the Dawho river, where the *Planter* was hotly and severely fired upon; also at Rockville, John's Island, and other places. Afterwards he was ordered back to Port Royal, whence he piloted the fleet up Broad river to Pocotaligo, where a very severe battle ensued. Captain Smalls was the pilot of the monitor *Keokuk,* Captain Ryan, in the memorable attack on Fort Sumter, on the afternoon of the seventh of April, 1863. In this attack the *Keokuk* was struck ninety-six times, nineteen shots passing through her. She retired from the engagement only to sink on the next morning, near Light House Inlet. Captain Smalls left her just before she went down, and was taken with the remainder of the crew on board of the *Ironside.* The next day the fleet returned to Hilton Head.

When General Gillmore took command, Smalls became pilot in the quartermaster's department in the expedition on Morris Island. He was then stationed as pilot of the *Stono,* where he remained until the United States troops took possession of the south end of Morris Island, when he was put in charge of Light House Inlet as pilot.

Upon one occasion, in December, 1863, while the *Planter,* then under command of Captain Nickerson, was sailing through Folly Island Creek, the Confederate batteries at Secessionville opened a very hot fire upon her. Captain Nickerson became demoralized, and left the pilot-house and secured himself in the coal-bunker. Smalls was on the deck, and finding out that the captain had deserted his post, entered the pilot-house, took command of the boat, and carried her safely out of the reach of the guns. For this conduct he was promoted by order of General Gillmore, commanding the Department of the South, to the rank of captain, and was ordered to act as captain of the *Planter,* which was used as a supply-boat along the coast until the end of the war.[138]

After the war was over, Robert Smalls really got busy crusading for his people! But first he returned to his birthplace, Beaufort, South Carolina and purchased the house he grew up in as a slave on 511 Prince Street.[139] Now a resident of South Carolina, Robert Smalls ran for and was elected to the South Carolina House of Representatives in 1868 which marked the beginning of his political career. If you do the math, in a course of SIX YEARS, this man went from a slave to a member of the South Carolina House of Representatives! And he wasn't done yet! In 1870 he filled a

---

[138] Simmons, 168-9.
[139] The Robert Smalls House was declared a National Historic Landmark in 1970's.

vacant seat in the South Carolina Senate and in 1872 he was formally elected into the same position, which he served until 1874, and he still wasn't done! In 1875, the Honorable Captain Robert Smalls was elected to the 44th United States Congress! And he still wasn't done as he was also elected to the 45th, 47th, 48th AND 49th CONGRESSES often beating White opponents for the post! So for almost ten years straight in the late 1800's, a former Black slave represented the great state of South Carolina in Congress! And you, more likely than not, knew NOTHING about him! And you might have a hard time believing it now as you've been persuaded to assume every post-1865 Black man in the South couldn't leave out of the house at night for fear of being lynched. And here you have Robert Smalls successfully running for and being elected as the Congressional representative of a southern state for several Congressional sessions!

And while he was Congressman, he consistently stood in defense of Black people. The August 1, 1876 Boston Daily Advertiser included an article that stated "Hon. Robert Smalls of South Carolina, who bravely defended his race against the mean attack of Sunset Cox a few days ago in the house, is one of the best representatives of the colored race in official position..."[140] The Honorable Robert Smalls was a slave with swag if ever there was one. You should spread the word of his accomplishments so he is not forgotten in the annals of history. Here is our beloved Brother:

---

[140] "Congressman Smalls of South Carolina," Boston Daily Advertiser, Aug. 1, 1876. 2.

Figure 56 War hero, Navy Captain, member of S.C. House of Representatives, member of S.C. Senate, FIVE-TIME U.S. Congressman and slave with swag, the Honorable Robert Smalls.

Blanche K. Bruce

Blanche Kelso Bruce was born a slave in 1841 in Prince Edward County, Virginia. He remained a slave until the outbreak of the civil war. As a slave, Blanche received some basic education from the tutor of his enslaver's son, which he put to use in Kansas and Missouri after the war. Instead of wondering what additional education would do for him, Blanche relocated to Oberlin, Ohio to attend Oberlin College. He only attended one course before leaving school and eventually headed to Mississippi to pursue other endeavors.[141]

Mississippi felt like home to young Blanche. He worked hard, purchased some land and got involved in local politics. His hard work coupled with his dominating physical appearance got him elected Sergeant-at-Arms of the State of Mississippi in 1870. As Sergeant-at-Arms, Blanche provided security at political meetings. Now, some men, particularly a former slave who was hired in part due to his physical size and ability to labor, might have taken offense to the suggestion that he work to protect men who were of the same hue as his former enslaver. But Blanche was smart. He was smart enough to realize the opportunity his new position afforded him. He aptly executed his duties and intelligently "made use of this close contact with leading men of that State to better develope [sp] the 'judgment, tact and executive ability which have so signally characterized his after life.'"[142] Now did some of his fellow Brothers and Sisters, particularly those who were also formerly bonded in slavery, label him a sell-out for providing security for White Mississippi aristocrats? Maybe, but Blanche didn't care. He knew that position was simply a means to an end. He also knew he would one day use his affiliation with those same White aristocrats to improve the plight of his people, despite their supposed disapproval of his current position.

Within a year of his Sergeant-at-Arms selection, Blanche K. Bruce was appointed Bolivar County (Mississippi) Assessor of Taxes. And a year after that, he was selected as SHERIFF of Bolivar County, and he performed those duties in addition to his Assessor duties! Yes, a Black man, who was a

---

[141] Simmons, 699.
[142] Simmons, 700.

Slaves With Swag

former slave, was SHERIFF of a Mississippi County in 1872! If you have problems believing that, then your brain will not be able to grasp the rest of Mr. Bruce's accomplishments.

Mr. Bruce slowly but surely worked his way up the Mississippi political ladder. Later in 1872, Mr. Bruce became an elected member of the Board of Levee Commissioners of the Mississippi River. And we all know how important the group can be after the Hurricane Katrina fiasco. All of these local and regional political appointments were preparing Mr. Bruce for the big stage. In February of 1874, the Mississippi Legislature, comprised mostly of southern White men, elected former slave Blanche Kelso Bruce to represent them in the U.S. Senate chamber and in March of 1875, Mr. Bruce started his term as U.S. Senator. IF YOU DON'T BELIEVE IT, then please go to http://www.senate.gov and type the man's name in the search box. He was a slave with swag and his work still was not done.

The Honorable Blanche K. Bruce served as Senator from 1875 to 1881. And during this time, while he was in his most influential position, he lobbied the hardest on behalf of his people. His record as a Senator speaks for itself:

- Lobbied on behalf of P.B.S. Pinchback who was another Black man that was elected to the Senate, but his election was contested.
- Lobbied the government to give larger land grants and tax-free clothing to Black Americans who migrated west.
- Lobbied for the desegregation of the U.S. Army.
- Lobbied for Senate inquiry into corruption and violence that took place during the 1875 Mississippi elections.
- Lobbied against discrimination experienced by Black Civil War Veteran's heirs who were denied their hero's pension payments.
- Chaired a committee to investigate corruption and incompetence at the Freedman's Savings and Trust Company.

- Lobbied for the investigation of discrimination and harassment against Black West Point cadet Johnson C. Whittaker.[143]

Think of the strength, fortitude and self confidence it took for a former slave to operate on the highest level of the Federal government only about 20 years after he was freed from slavery! Think about it! Mr. Bruce did not have the benefit of a hearty education, internships or other formal training. But what he did have was God-given ability which trumps any man-made training any day of the week. Mr. Bruce was so confident in his abilities that he competed for the nomination of Vice President of the United States! In 1880 Senator Bruce teamed with Senator James G. Blaine to seek the Republican nomination for Vice President and President of the United States of America, respectively. If you thought it was a feat for President Obama to run in 2008, what kind of work do you think Blanche Bruce had to put in to run 128 YEARS EARLIER IN 1880! Opponents accused Obama of not being a U.S. citizen, what in the world do you think they accused Mr. Bruce of being given his former status as slave? And in case you're having a difficult time believing a Black man who was a former slave ran for the Vice Presidential nomination in 1880, here is an article from the May 28, 1880 Herald of Kansas newspaper supporting both candidates:

---

[143] Black Americans In Congress, http://www.baic.house.gov, December 2011.

OUR TICKET

For President,

JAS. G. BLAINE.

Of Maine.

For Vice-President,

B. K. BRUCE.

Of Mississippi

Friday Morning, May 28.

LET the ticket read James G Blaine and Blanche K. Bruce

HURRAH for Blanche K. Bruce, the coming Negro of America.

LET the colored delegates remember that they are expected to vote solid for Blanche K. Bruce next Wednesday.

WITH James G. Blaine and B. K. Bruce as their standard bearers, the Republicans will march to victory next fall.

A LIVELY fight will be made next Wednesday in the National Convention to place the name of B. K. Bruce, of Mississippi, for the second place on the National ticket. Such men as J. Milton Turner, Frederick Douglass, and others of prominence will be there and do all that lies in their power to have some recognition accorded the million colored voters of this country. The prospect for success is very bright.

Figure 57 American newspaper documentation of a slave with swag.[144]

[144] Herald of Kansas, May 28, 1880. 2.

Although the Blaine-Bruce ticket did not get the nomination, that did not stop Mr. Bruce from being a relevant political powerhouse and achieving greater heights. In May 1881, President James Garfield appointed Blanche K. Bruce Register of the U.S. Treasury. The Register was the bookkeeper of United States funding and as Register, Mr. Bruce's signature was affixed on United States currency effectively validating that currencies' value. Don't believe that? Well here are facsimiles of a few of those bills signed by Blanche K. Bruce!

Figure 58 Blanche K. Bruce authorized $1 bill series.

Figure 59 Blanche K. Bruce authorized $2 series bill.

Slaves With Swag

Figure 60 Blanche K. Bruce authorized $5 series bill.

Figure 61 Blanche K. Bruce authorized $10 series bill.

Figure 62 Blanche K. Bruce authorized $20 series bill.

Figure 63 Blanche K. Bruce authorized $50 series bill.

Figure 64 Blanche K. Bruce authorized $500 series bill.

The Honorable Blanche Kelso Bruce held his first appointment as Register of the Treasury from 1881 to 1885 and his second appointment by President William McKinley from 1897 until his death on March 17, 1898. The proof of this man's accomplishments is irrefutable. In ADDITION to all his other duties, the Honorable Blanche K. Bruce served as Recorder of Deeds in Washington D.C. (see below article from the front page of the January 1, 1890 Philadelphia Inquirer) and sat on the Board of Trustees at Howard University.

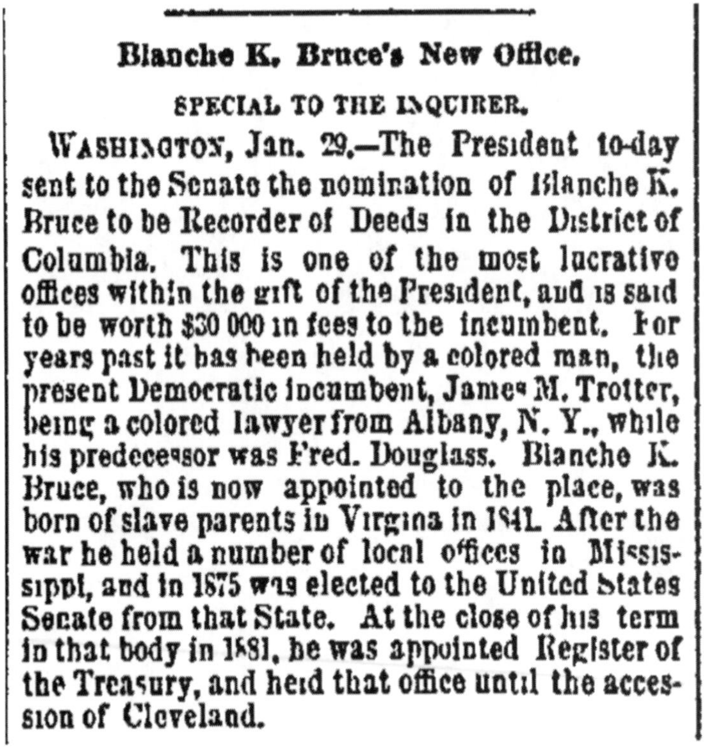

Blanche K. Bruce's New Office.

SPECIAL TO THE INQUIRER.

WASHINGTON, Jan. 29.—The President to-day sent to the Senate the nomination of Blanche K. Bruce to be Recorder of Deeds in the District of Columbia. This is one of the most lucrative offices within the gift of the President, and is said to be worth $30 000 in fees to the incumbent. For years past it has been held by a colored man, the present Democratic incumbent, James M. Trotter, being a colored lawyer from Albany, N. Y., while his predecessor was Fred. Douglass. Blanche K. Bruce, who is now appointed to the place, was born of slave parents in Virginia in 1841. After the war he held a number of local offices in Mississippi, and in 1875 was elected to the United States Senate from that State. At the close of his term in that body in 1881, he was appointed Register of the Treasury, and held that office until the accession of Cleveland.

Figure 65 American newspaper article that documents the actions of a slave with swag.[145]

Since the Honorable Blanche Kelso Bruce was such a prominent figure, his nomination by President McKinley made the front page of the Philadelphia Inquirer and many other publications. The article mentions that the fees for his position would equate to about $30,000 in 1890 currency. That same $30,000 would equate to about $700,000 in today's currency. The Honorable Blanche Kelso Bruce was truly a slave with swag.

---

[145] Philadelphia Inquirer, January 1, 1890. 1.

Figure 66 Here is the Black man whose signature gave American currency value. He went from slavery to the Senate, the Honorable Blanche Kelso Bruce.[146]

---

[146] The last home Mr. Bruce owned was located at 909 M Street NW, Washington D.C. and similar to the Robert Smalls House, the Blanche K. Bruce House is on the National Registry of Historic Places.

7 The Messages

There are a few messages you should take away from this text. The obvious one is every Black person born before 1865 was not necessarily a slave. The next obvious message is Black slaves fought, were educated, had freedom and money and a great many of them had swag. The not so obvious messages are as follows: 1) Slavery Was About Money; 2) There is Much More to Black History, White History Too; and 3) Protect Your Investment. Let's break them down.

Message #1: Slavery Was About Money

When the first White/European settlers arrived in this country, they realized there was a lot of work to be done, both physical and mental. The physical work included cultivating the land, constructing roads and buildings, growing and harvesting crops, raising and processing animals, making clothes, etc. The mental work included developing and implementing the new world's economic, political, religious, social and EDUCATIONAL systems that would govern the people. Somewhere along the way it was decided that Black/African labor was the most effective and efficient means of getting the physical work completed, and thus began the trans-Atlantic slave trade. Subsequently, it was also decided that European brain power would do the mental work.

Now, logic demands that it would have been in the Whites' best interest to organize the political, religious, social and EDUCATIONAL systems in a manner that would perpetuate the building of the country, particularly its economy. In other words, it was in the Whites' best interest to strategically develop the governing systems in a manner that would perpetuate the continued enslavement of Black people. If the White people in power did not consistently perpetuate the enslavement of Black people, then the White people in power would have had to do all that physical work in addition to the mental work, and that obviously wasn't happening![147] So what did they do? They created and embedded the concept of Black or Negro inferiority in the country's governing systems to give the impression that Black people were of a low level of humanity and intelligence and were only capable of performing manual labor.

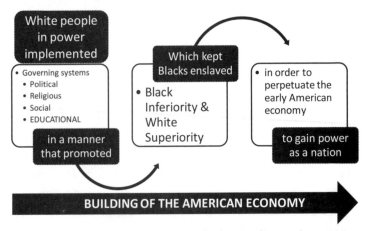

Figure 67 The White people in power implemented governing systems (economic, political, religious, social and EDUCATIONAL) that vehemently promoted the concept of Black inferiority and White superiority in order to manipulate the Black slaves to continue to be slaves. This manipulation perpetuated the early American economy and created wealth for the nation.

The Black inferiority concept provided some sort of moral cushion for White people and helped to convince Black people that is was okay for them to be slaves.

---

[147] A distinction needs to be made here between the Whites who were wealthy and powerful (let's call them the 'haves') and the poor Whites who had no power (let's call them the 'have nots'). The White people discussed here are the White 'haves'. There were plenty of White 'have nots' who worked side-by-side with the Black slaves performing the physical work. Many of them were first generation European immigrants. Further detail on the White 'have nots' will be provided later in this chapter.

Now, the fact that White people in power designed the governing systems to promote Black inferiority does not necessarily mean they honestly felt Black people were inferior. It was strictly business to a certain extent. The heart of the matter wasn't one so-called race believing it was superior to another so-called race. The heart of the matter was the growth of a nation, particularly the wealth of the nation.

Enslavers' creation and promotion of the Negro inferiority complex wasn't the first time mental manipulation was used to keep a group of people in an oppressed state. Let's take a few minutes to examine the industry that created this model, which also happens to be the world's oldest profession, prostitution. The relationship between a pimp and a prostitute, better known as a 'ho,' was extremely similar to that between enslaver and slave. The ho does all the work, while the pimp collects all the dough. When that ho comes in from a hard nights' work, does the pimp pat her on the back and tell her what a great job she did out there on the stroll, and rub her feet and thank her for sacrificing her body for him? No. WHAT DOES HE TELL HER? He tells her she ain't nothing but a low-down, dirty dog! He teaches her how ugly, ignorant and helpless she is. He constantly reminds her that she would never make it in the world without him and no ho has ever amounted to anything but a ho.

WHY DOES HE TELL HER THAT? Simple baby, so her self-esteem remains low enough to keep that ho strollin' tough. The pimp MUST make the ho feel as though she's nothing, so she'll continue to allow strange men to violate her body and turn over the money to him. He must consistently keep her self-esteem low enough to violate the direction of God so she can perform her duties and make 'his' money. The pimp has to convince her that she needs him to survive, in order to keep her from realizing that he really needs her. She holds all the power, but his consistent, malicious rants

Slaves With Swag

about her insignificance intentionally blinds her and reduces her self-esteem to rubbish. It has nothing to do with love or hate, it's about business. Deep down, the pimp may even recognize that a ho is actually more intelligent than he is and maybe even superior to him in certain aspects of humanity. But at the end of the day, he would never admit that and instead will talk a ho down because he knows no self-respecting, high self-esteemed woman would sell her body then give the money to somebody else. And until that ho figures out the pimp's game, she will forever remain a ho.

The slaves of this country were very similar to the ho in the example. The slaves sacrificed their bodies and put in the work, while the enslavers cashed the checks. So if the enslavers are the pimps, how do they need to make the slaves feel about themselves in order to keep them enslaved? RIGHT! Like ignorant, ugly, stupid, funky, shameful, cowardly, low-down dirty dogs! And that's exactly what the enslavers did. They did it during their daily interaction with the slaves and they made sure the systems they developed and implemented (political, social, religious, and EDUCATIONAL) reinforced the Negro inferiority message and created an inferiority complex in Black people in America. Once the system got going, the powers that be were forced to promote the message of Black inferiority to see their dream of a rich and powerful American country come to fruition. Slavery represented free labor. For those of you who own businesses, imagine what your financial statements would look like if you didn't have to pay any of your employees salary, your portion of their health insurance nor your portion of their taxes! You'd be rich in no time.

Some of the White people obviously really believed Blacks were inferior because they wrote about it and openly spoke about it, but a great many had to be well aware of the African origin of human civilization and the African's contribution to human development in the Nile Valley.

Regardless of either case, the White people in power were forced to support the message of Black inferiority to accomplish the goal of GREEN superiority.

The remnants of this early educational manipulation might be the reason why you learned primarily about pre-1865 Black people who were violently enslaved (Category 1) and not about the Brothers and Sisters mentioned in this book (Category 2). No one knows the true answer for sure, and this is just a theory as it would take a lifetime of research to get to the root of it. But the fact remains, the foundation of our education system, specifically the History curriculum, is skewed. It's skewed because it was developed during a time when it was perfectly acceptable for ANYONE on the radio, in the lecture hall, in the newspapers, in the street, etc. to promote the idea of Negro inferiority. The powers that be allowed society to go in that direction at that time in order to build the American economy, but things have changed significantly since then. The powers that be now have made it clear that it is not okay to openly promote the idea of Black inferiority anymore. There also have been attempts to correct the History curriculum, i.e Black History Month, etc. that should be recognized. But at the end of the day, the History curriculum tree was cocked-to-the-side when it was planted a few hundred years ago and it will forever remain with a lean. See, if you plant a tree at an angle and the roots mature while that tree is at an angle, there is nothing that you can ever do that will make that tree upright. You can trim some branches and stake it here or there to give the illusion of erectness, but the roots are skewed so the tree will be forever skewed, especially since it had more than 400 years to mature at a slant.

Instead of attempting to make a crooked tree erect, we will be much better off planting new trees of knowledge when it comes to Black History. Many Black scholars (and non-Black scholars who write from the Black perspective) have planted those new trees for some time now. There are literally thousands of books on Black History that shed a much more positive light on what we have done as a people.[148] And those new trees represent our cultural self-knowledge as a people.[149] History written from the Black perspective will give Black people Knowledge of Self! History from the Black perspective has Black people at its center. You, Brother and Sister are the primary topic instead of the secondary. It provides a history of your people and how other people related to you instead of the other way around.

We must supplement one side of the story (i.e. one perspective) with another in order to get the whole picture. Aren't there two sides to every story, sometimes three? As you very well know, three people can witness the exact same event, on the exact same day, same time, same sunlight, same angle, same everything, yet interpret that event three different ways. When it comes to history, no one alive today was there to personally witness events of the past. Since that is the case, all modern historians are forced to interpret somebody else's interpretation of past events which further complicates matters. That complication demands you hear (read) more than just one side of the story in order to get the whole picture, especially when the side you heard for the first 18 years of your life was purposely skewed at its genesis for the purposes of financial gain. Besides, it would be foolish for the descendant of a ho to depend solely on the descendant of a pimp for the historical information required to build her cultural self-esteem and sense of self wealth. So those of us who are descendants of slaves[150] must take the initiative to learn who we are on our own accord and somewhat

---

[148] The bibliography of this book would be a great place to start.

[149] Please note the use of the word culture here and not race. There is only one race, the human race, and we all exercise different cultures within that race.

[150] Remember, not all of us are descendants of slaves as 488,070 Black people were free as of the 1860 census.

independent of the descendants of our former enslavers to make sure we don't get pimped again. If you know who The O'Jays are, then you already know what the love of money will make people do to one another.

2. There's MUCH More To Black History (White History Too)

Black people have a deep rooted history on this Earth: an uncivilized history that began about six million years ago with the Ardipithecus kadabba[151] in Ethiopia; and a highly civilized history that began about 3200 B.C. with the unification of the Northern and Southern Kingdoms by Pharaoh Narmer in ancient Egypt. Now with thousands of years of post-civilized Black History behind us, why do we focus so much on this short 200 to 300 years we were enslaved?

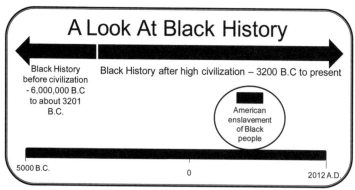

Figure 68 The focus of your Black History education.

You know why. The educational system and the History curriculum was developed during a time when the powers that be were forced to push the message of Negro inferiority to the general society to perpetuate the economy. What better way to do that than by placing gargantuan emphasis on the period when Black people were slaves and pretty much ignoring everything that happened before then?

---

[151] Ardipithecus kadabba is the name given to humanoid remains discovered in Ethiopia by an Ethiopian archeologist Dr. Yohannes Haile-Selassie. Simply search for it or him for more information.

123

Slaves With Swag

The curriculum left you to ASSUME native Africans were brutes and savages that could only amount to being good slaves outside of the 'jungle', but that couldn't be further from the truth. Again, Black History, after the point where Africans were exercising high levels of civilization, began about 3200 B.C., which is over 5,200 years ago, yet the majority of your education about Black people focused on that short 200-300 year period in time when Africans were enslaved in America. It is strongly suggested that you read some ancient African History from the Black perspective! It will literally blow your mind. Anything by Dr. Yosef ben-Jochannan, Dr. John Henrik Clarke, Joel A. Rogers, Cheikh Anta Diop, John G. Jackson or Ishakamusa Barashango is highly recommended.

Detailed data and facts that prove the African origin of human civilization is very important information for any Black person. Over 4,700 years of Black History before Africans became American slaves was/is totally ignored in the classroom and in general American society. The rest of the story on African History will eradicate that negative imagery of ancient Africans (half-naked, cannibalistic, yipping and yelping savages) you have floating around in your head. Please read it!

Your general education also left you to ASSUME the only people on Earth to have ever been enslaved were Africans in America and that simply is not true. American enslavement of the African is the most well-known slavery system because its more recent than other major slave systems and we all were taught it for the first 18 years of our lives, but by no means is it the only. In fact, one of the most ruthless forms of slavery our Earth has ever seen was the enslavement of White children. They were used to power the industrial revolution here in America and as chimney sweeps in both Europe and America, the latter duty being particularly vicious. Don't believe it? A photographer named Lewis W.

Hine traveled America and documented horrific cases of child labor in American factories. Look him up and see for yourself. Also, the use of young White boys as chimney sweeps, better known as climbing boys, is very well documented. Poor White children were forced to sweep the soot out of the chimneys of well-to-do European and American homes mostly because they were the only ones small enough to fit down the stacks. Their small stature though still did not prevent many from becoming stuck in the soot and creosote filled chimneys and suffocating to death. Some were burned alive and countless members of them contracted lung cancer, soot wart (which was cancer of the scrotum), and blindness. Keep in mind the average age of these poor enslaved souls was 5 – 12. If they survived their daily ordeals, and made it out of adolescence, many of them died in their twenties due to the cancer. An English poet by the name of William Blake wrote a stirring poem dedicated to them in 1789 titled *The Chimney Sweeper (Songs of Innocence)*. Feel free to look up the poem and other documentation of these poor, enslaved babies.[152]

In addition to the children, grown White people were enslaved here in America by White enslavers. Many of them worked shoulder-to-shoulder with the Black slaves! The main difference between the two was White slaves were called servants instead of slaves. DON'T BELIEVE THAT? Well, please read this June 8, 1884 article ran in the Cincinnati Commercial Tribune:

[152] Hopefully the Master of us all, the Almighty God dealt with the men and women who both enslaved and employed these children. Only a beast would send a five year-old child down a toxin filled chimney for any other purpose than to escape danger.

WHITE SLAVES SOLD.

Eighteen Unhappy Paupers Auctioned Off to the Highest Bidders.

In the town of St. George, the seat of Tucker County, in the heart of Cheat Mountain, over-looking the beautiful Cheat River, stood eighteen wretched beings Friday before a crowd of some six hundred people. The crowd was gathered before the little Court-house, and included farmers, clergymen and towns-people.

These eighteen human beings, some crying, others laughing, and among them an idiotic girl suffering from a scrofulous disease, who jabbered and grinned, were paupers, and they were, under the law of the State, to be sold for the term of one year to the highest bidder

Promptly at 10 o'clock the crowd gathered in front of the Court-house and inspected the paupers, while the town boys on the outskirts of the throng jeered and tormented the un-fortunates, this being taken as a matter of course and something that no person thought of stopping. Presently the Sheriff of the coun-ty mounted the horse block, that relic of the dark days of slavery in ante-bellum times, and read "the order of the court."

Then the auctioneer, a stout, jolly faced in-dividual, mounted the block, and, making a jesting remark which caused the crowd to roar with laughter, announced that the "goods are divided into two classes, able-bodied and in-valids," and asked for bids

The first to step upon the block was an old man seventy years of age Turning him around for the better inspection of the bidders, the auctioneer began. "Now, gentlemen," said he, "here you have a fine man. He is sound, solid and gentle as a kitten. He is good for a big day's work. How much am I offered?" The old fellow looked anxiously at the crowd of bidders as the amounts offered were outbid. Finally he was sold to a man named John Anderson for $26, who, after paying his money, took the old fellow, who looked sad and weary, and sighed heavily as he went away with him.

Among the group of paupers was a beautiful little girl of ten years, who cried bitterly because she had to leave the family to whom she had been sold the previous year. She had neither father nor mother, or, if she had, they had thrown her adrift when an infant. She had not even a name, and the auctioneer facetiously dubbed her "Sally," whereat his listeners laughed immoderately. She sold for $3 50, and her purchaser was a minister of the gospel.

One of the most pitiful sights ever seen was that of the next pauper to be sold. She was an old woman, and it was her first year as a pauper. Perhaps she had once been rich in this world's goods and had a happy home. At all events, she had supported herself till the present time, and the question of her past was known only to herself. No one else knew, no one cared. She was led to the block crying as though her heart would break. When she stepped upon it she wailed in her anguish: "My God, I wish that I could die. My husband and son were killed in the army. Oh, if I could only die!" She was sold to the keeper of a boarding-house at a logging camp for $7.

The idiotic girl was sold to a hard-looking mountaineer for the sum of sixty cents per week.

As the next part of the human goods and chattels stepped upon the block it showed the white, curly locks of an aged colored man, who laughed as he looked over the throng with his good-humored and jolly eyes. "I golly," said he, as he glanced around, 'dis yer is like ol' times, bress my soul." He was sold to a farmer for $11.

> The sale aggregated $113 for the "able-bodied" paupers and an average price of thirty-two cents per week for the invalids At the conclusion of the sale the jolly auctioneer, with a parting jest to the crowd, stepped from his stand and, entering the hotel, refreshed himself after his fatiguing duties. The purchasers with their "bargains," as some of them termed the unfortunates whom they had bought, started off homeward
>
> The stories of cruelty to these people are numerous and beyond question or doubt. They are worked to their utmost capacity They are fed on refuse, made to sleep in barns, have to go barefooted for ten months in the year, and are whipped, and whipped savagely on the slightest pretext. The tales of immorality are frequent and too often true The children are allowed to grow up without education, and it is said some of them do not even know that a God exists They contract diseases which are neglected, for in many cases medical aid is denied them. These poor wretches, in addition to their other sorrows, are the butt and jeer of every person not a pauper. They are looked on as a piece of goods with only a money value, varied in accordance with their ability to perform manual labor.

Figure 69 American newspaper documentation of White slaves i.e. servants. June 6, 1884 Cincinnati Commercial Tribune.[153]

IF YOU STILL DON'T BELIEVE IT, THEN GO TO YOUR LOCAL LIBRARY AND ASK THEM TO PULL A MICROFICHE COPY OF THE PAPER. You'll find the article on page 15.[154]

Even before White people were enslaved in America, they were enslaved in Europe. Bishop James W. Hood who

[153] Cincinnati Commercial Tribune, June 8, 1884, 15.
[154] The details of White slavery is beyond the bounds of this text, but many works exist on the topic the most prominent being *White Servitude in the Colony of Virginia* written by James Curtis Ballagh in 1895.

was born a free Black man in Kennett Township, Pennsylvania in 1831 (Category 3 pre-1865 Black person) was forced to remind one of his opponents of that at a South Carolina political convention. Bishop Hood was a delegate at the convention and the opponent made reference to Black inferiority during his disagreement with one of Rev. Hood's measures. The good Bishop replied as follows:

> The gentleman from Orange remarked last night that his race has always occupied a position more elevated than the rest of mankind. I am astonished at that young man that he has no more regard for his reputation as a historian than to assert such a ridiculous fallacy in the hearing of intelligent gentlemen in the noonday splendor of the nineteenth century. Does he not know that his ancestors, the ancient Britons, were in bondage in ancient Rome, in the days of Julius Cæsar, and ever since that day? Mr. Chairman, the worst that has ever been said of my people was that they were too ignorant to be anything but slaves; but of the Britons it was said that they were too ignorant even to be slaves. A friend of Julius Cæsar, writing to him, urged him not to bring slaves from Britain, for they were so ignorant that they could not be taught music. Now I have never heard it said of colored people that they were too ignorant to sing.[155]

And here is Bishop James W. Hood. He founded countless churches in North Carolina, South Carolina and Virginia, was agent of the State Board of Education and assistant superintendent of public instruction, as well as assistant superintendent of the Freedmen's Bureau.

---

[155] Simmons, 137.

Slaves With Swag

Figure 70 Bishop James Walker Hood. A never enslaved pre-1865 Black man (Category 3). His educational letters included D.D. (Doctor of Divinity) and LL.D. (Doctor of Law).

Believe it or not, slavery goes on right now today. Unfortunately, this statement is applicable whether you are reading this book during the 21st century or the 121st century simply because slavery is a human behavior and as long as there are humans, there will be slavery. If you don't believe slavery is in existence today (early 21st century), do a little research on the term 'human trafficking.' The name changes, but the institution remains the same.

So that being said Brothers and Sisters, you need to know Black people were not the only enslaved people of this Earth. Since humanity has existed, people have enslaved other people for financial gains, regardless of color or culture and ALL OF THEM WERE WRONG! Focusing Black History on the short 300 year period of your enslavement was about money. Thankfully, we've culturally matured enough now to not only know our history runs much deeper than that, but to pull the details to validate that feeling you had deep down inside when the topic of slavery was brought up. The feeling that stirred you to say 'I couldn't have been nobody's slave.' It's that same feeling the Slaves with Swag mentioned in this book had when they made their moves. It's okay to recognize the enslavement of some of your forefathers. In fact, it's good to be conscious of the who, what, why, when, where and how it happened for the sole purpose of making sure it doesn't happen again. It is not okay, however, for you to totally ignore the other 4,700 years of your history before you were enslaved. It simply does not make sense.

3. Protect Your Investment

So now you know the truth. Slaves and former slaves achieved heights you could never have imagined and that information wasn't presented to you in school. Are you angry? Does that fact infuriate you? Well, don't let it. The enslavement of our ancestors wasn't personal, it was strictly business. Don't be bitter toward White people. No White person alive today enslaved a Black person. Now SOME of their ancestors did, but not as many as you think. The 1790 census reported a total number of 405,475 White families in the United States with 47,664 of them holding slaves. Even if you ASSUME all the slaves they held were Black that only equates to about 12% of all White families in 1790 who held slaves. Now, it's highly unlikely you have the innate ability to arbitrarily identify the descendants of that 12%. Even if you could, what's the value in holding the great-great-great grandson accountable for the crime of an ancestor? Besides, COUNTLESS White men, women and children have assisted Black slaves all along the way. Scores of Whites like John Vandavall, John Qunicy Adams, Nelson Nicholson, Belva A. Lockwood, Nancy White and Anthony Benezet, all mentioned in this book, played a major role in turning Category 1 Slaves to Category 2. One example worth mentioning involves our Slave with Swag Blanche Kelso Bruce who was elected Senator in 1874. When new Senators took their oath in the Chamber, the tradition was the senior Senator from the same state would escort the new Senator down the aisle. Senator

Slaves With Swag

Alcorn was the senior Senator for Mississippi when Mr. Bruce took his oath. Here is that story as told by Mr. Bruce:

> When I came up to the Senate I knew no one except Senator Alcorn, who was my colleague. When the names of the new Senators were called out for them to go up and take the oath, all the others except myself were escorted by their colleagues. Mr. Alcorn made no motion to escort me, but was buried behind a newspaper, and I concluded I would go it alone. I had got about half way up the aisle when a tall gentleman stepped up to me and said: 'Excuse me, Mr. Bruce, I did not until this moment see that you were without an escort. Permit me. My name is Conkling,' and he linked his arm in mine and we marched up to the desk together. I took the oath and then he escorted me back to my seat. Later in the day, when they were fixing up the committees, he asked me if any one was looking after my interests, and upon my informing him that there was not and that I was myself more ignorant of my rights in the matter, he volunteered to attend to it, and as a result I was placed on some very good committees and shortly afterwards got a chairmanship. I have always felt very kindly towards Mr. Conkling since, and always shall.[156]

And here is a picture of the Honorable Roscoe Conkling, friend and mentor of the Honorable Blanche K. Bruce:

Figure 71 New York Senator Roscoe Conkling.

The friendship between Blanche Bruce and Roscoe Conkling lasted for years. Mr. Conkling mentored Mr. Bruce in and outside the Senate chamber and Mr. Bruce developed such a healthy respect for Mr. Conkling as to name his only

---

[156] Simmons, 703.

son after him, Roscoe Conkling Bruce! Understand, the same way you can't assume all pre-1865 Black people were slaves, you also cannot assume all pre-1865 White people were enslavers or thought lowly of Black people. Mr. Conkling is just one shining example of early American White men who helped Blacks conquer their burdens, so please don't waste your time and energy harvesting malice for White people. Your malice may be against the ancestors of one of these upright White men that assisted one of your ancestors.

So what about your history teachers? You certainly should have some malice towards them, right? After all, they were the ones who withheld important cultural information from you, right? Wrong. We should NOT be bitter toward current educators or even the education system. Nobody that is here and alive today was around to plant that tree at an angle 400 years ago. When they were born, that tree was already 200 feet tall. Current educators are not at the root (of the problem), they're more like leaves of the branches trying to prosper under the same system we are. Don't be bitter and harbor hate. It will only make you physically, mentally and emotionally sick. Don't get mad, get even by correcting the nonsense you learned with Knowledge of Self and teaching others. Don't let your children come up under a leaning tree. It's dangerous. Give them fruit from our trees of knowledge.

Lastly, **DON'T BE BITTER TOWARD <u>YOUR COUNTRY</u>!** Love your country, our country, the United States of America. After all, Black people played a critical role in its rise, so the descendants of those Black people should reap some benefit of the work of their forefathers. But you can't do that if bitterness is blocking your vision. Love your home, which is Africa, but also love your country, which is America, she would not be without the blood, sweat and tears of all the Black people mentioned in this book and the millions more for which there simply was not enough room. The Rev. B.W. Arnett said it best in his speech on The Black Laws of Ohio.

Slaves With Swag

The topic was colonization which was a term used to describe the back to Africa movement in the 1800s. The good Reverend had this to say:

Now, in the name of the intelligence of the race, I give notice to all concerned that we do not intend to go [back to Africa] unless it is of our own free will and accord. We cannot go without taking some of the glory of this country with us. We cannot go unless we have a settlement with this Nation. We cannot go unless we receive indemnity at the hands of the government. We would desire to take everything that belongs to us with us: and therefore we must have the bones of our fathers, the tears of our mothers, the sighs of our sisters, the groans of our brothers, the blood of the wounded and the life of the dead, in order that we may be able to carry our memories with us, and forget the wrongs of the years and the sufferings of the centuries. We must have a settlement for the years of unpaid labor in the South. We want to collect in some huge cask the tears wrung from the hearts of the bondsmen by the lash. We will not leave this country as long as there remains a bone of the soldiers of the Revolution in the soil. No, sir; we will stay here until every bone of the fugitives of other years is returned, with its flesh, to its family and friends, and the reunited families shall be honored with the blessings of the new day of freedom.

Ask us to go from this land with the record of the soldiers of the three great wars shining with glory to our race! No, sir; you might as well understand it first as last, we are NOT going. While the memory of the heroes of Port Hudson and "Milliken's Bend" is being sung by our children, and while the soldiers of the war assemble around the camp fire and relate how

We led the Union soldier,
When fleeing from his foe;
We brought him through the mountains,
Where white men dare not go.
Our hoe cake and our cabbage
And pork we freely gave,
That this old flag might be sustained;
Now let it brightly wave.

Let us remember the deeds of valor of the heroes of the war, and preserve the jewel of liberty in the family of freedom. We say unto you that, as God reigns in the world, we will not leave nor forsake you: for your country will be our country;

we will feel the same pride in its mountains of iron, silver and gold as you do. We will feel as much pride in its valleys, plains, lakes, rivers, trade, commerce, institutions of learning, manufacturing interests, and in its unparalleled advantages to the husbandman; and in all of these we glory with you.

We shall say of our country, our fathers' country: Where thou dwellest, I will dwell; where thou goest to school, I will go, whether in the log school-house at the cross-roads, or the high school on the avenue; thy preacher shall be my preacher, and I will be buried in the same graveyard with you--so help me God.[157]

Rev. Arnett was a Black man and he was NEVER a slave. He was born a free man in Brownsville, Fayette County, Pennsylvania in 1838. You probably never heard of him before now, but that's okay, don't get upset, you know him now. Here is our Brother:

Figure 72 Rev. B.W. Arnett. A never enslaved pre-1865 Black man (category 3). His name was mentioned in the February 5, 1887 Cleveland Gazette Robert Harlan article in this book.

---

[157] Simmons, 890-1.

Slaves With Swag

Black people belong here in America. After all, didn't God send us here? Didn't you know He sent ancient Africans here on their own vessels centuries before Europeans got here? Are you under the very false impression that the first time an African hit North America was in the belly of a slave ship? Absolutely not! How do we know that? Well take a look at what Europeans found when they got here:

Figure 73 One of the massive Olmec stone heads 'discovered' in what is now known as Mexico by European settlers.

Look at that prominent nose and those full lips! It would be difficult if not impossible to produce any larger or more Africanesque physical evidence of the African presence in America before our arrival here on anybody's slave ship. The statue's features are undeniably African![158] Please don't assume the only way we got here was on the slave ship! Africans sailed the ocean years before Columbus' great-great-great grandfather was born. Don't believe that either? Well, here is the barge of the great African Pharaoh Khufu. It is housed in an African museum and dates back to 2600 B.C, which is approximately 4,100 years before Christopher Columbus sailed in 1492 A.D.

---

[158] Please read Ivan Van Sertima's *They Came Before Columbus* for tons of evidence on the topic.

Figure 74 Pharaoh Khufu's Solar Barge which dates to 2600 B.C.

And here is a statue of Pharaoh Khufu himself.

Figure 75 African Pharaoh Khufu, owner of the Solar Barge and erecter of the Great Pyramid at Giza. Note the lips and the nose. Again, ancient African History from the Black perspective will blow your mind!

Brothers and Sisters, your people played a prominent role in the development of America. Think of the wealth Black people created for America. Money is time, and time is money. How much was the Black slaves' time worth? The 1860 census shows that there were 3,953,760 slaves that year. Assuming those slaves worked just eight hours a day, six days a week, 52 weeks a year totals 9,868,584,960 hours of work completed by slaves in the year 1860 alone. Now let's say that work yielded a modest profit of $2/hour. Using that conservative assumption, the slaves of 1860 generated some $19,737,169,920. That's well over $19 BILLION dollars and that's only one year's worth of work and only assumes eight hours of work per day. The calculations are loose, but the demonstration of net worth created by slave labor stands. Again, this number only represents ONE year of work and Black people were enslaved for a few hundred years! You do the math! Even prominent White authors recognized the contribution of Black people to our country. On page 45 of *A Refutation of Calumnies,* Edwin C. Holland summarized Alexander Hewatt as follows:

> Here then is a candid acknowledgment from one of the most scrupulous writers upon the subject of slavery, and who never touches upon it but with feelings of bitter and determined hostility, even while he admits its necessity, under some circumstances. The same reasons urged by him at the period when he wrote as to the necessity, therefore, of the use of Africans in the cultivation of this valuable staple, may now be urged with redoubled force. The country owes almost all its wealth and prosperity, and the revenue of the Union an immense increase in its fund, to the labor of this strong and hardy race.[159]

At the end of the day, Black people are heavily invested in OUR country, and as you can see, we're in DEEP! Take care of your investment Brothers and Sisters! It's an endowment from your forefathers. If you're Black, it would be a travesty to let your ancestors' sacrifice go for naught, because if your ancestors were slaves, and you're alive, they sacrificed plenty for their and ultimately your survival. Don't use your ancestors' enslavement as a crutch or an excuse for laziness. Don't let it hinder your progress. White people certainly don't let the fact that some of their people were enslaved slow them down, not one iota. Now granted, they didn't have the concept of White enslavement and White inferiority consistently jammed down their throats during their most impressionable years, but they persevere regardless. Don't let the fact that SOME of your people were enslaved for a short period of time stunt your growth. In fact, you shouldn't automatically assume you are the descendant of a slave!

---

[159] Holland, 45.

Remember that 488,070 Black people here in America were FREE as of 1860. You could very easily be one of their descendants! If you think about it, statistically speaking about 10-12% of Black Americans must be.

So for the other 88-90% of you who are the descendants of slaves, don't assume, your great, great, great ancestors were one of those 'gwine do dis, gwine do dat' Category 1 type of slave. There seemed to be a VERY thin line between a Category 1 and Category 2 slave and records suggest there were many more Category 2 type slaves than one would imagine. So, be proud of their accomplishments. Take pride in the fact that they fought like men and women. Take pride in the fact that they were educated despite their obstacles. Take pride in the fact that many of them operated as free men and women, worked for money and had the intestinal fortitude to foster deals with their enslaver to purchase their freedom and the freedom of their families! You can very easily be the descendant of one of the millions of Category 2 type slaves mentioned in this book, a fighting slave, an educated slave, a slave with freedom and money, a SLAVE WITH SWAG!

Even if you are a descendant of one of those Category 1 type slaves, the simple fact that you are here and alive with us gives you much to be proud of. Imagine the STRENGTH it took to live under those horrid conditions. Pull strength from their strength and take pride in the fact that they were tough enough to persevere under that pressure. Take pride in the fact that your enslaved ancestor had the internal, physical and mental strength to sustain the pressures of one of the worst slave systems our Earth has ever seen. Take pride in their existence the same way someone from Confederate heritage takes pride in their history despite the fact that Confederates lost the battle and the war.

It's quite obvious many of you are achieving, taking care of your children, bettering our national community despite our former bondage and that's fantastic. But don't think because you've achieved some level of success that you can coast. Keep striving! Before reading this text, you were forced to compare your current accomplishments with the ancestral heritage of Category 1 type slaves because that's all you knew. Now, how do you stack up against Category 2 slaves? You were previously under the false impression that the Black 'bar' of achievement was just above not being a slave because of what you were taught, but reading this book just raised your cultural achievement bar ten-fold. You have more work to do Brothers and Sisters. Be proud that you did a good job, but don't let your achievements to date be the pinnacle of your accomplishments. Use the energy the Creator gives you every day to achieve! And whatever your accomplishments are and will be, give thanks to the Creator and show appreciation of what He/She has bestowed upon you.

Contribute something that your descendents will benefit from 100 years from now. Spend your time wisely, not distracted by the traps set by the world capitalists. And note, those traps are set for ALL AMERICANS, not just Black Americans, so don't feel sorry for yourself and use your skin color as a crutch. It's the 21st century and skin color is not as relevant as it used to be say 50 years ago. Please recognize, skin color and differences in culture still play a prominent role in influencing **SOME** peoples' actions (Rest-In-Peace Trayvon Martin), but people in our country are reacting to skin color less and less as the generations pass. Eventually, the ultimate color that will influence peoples' actions is green, money green to be exact. That is not to say cultural bias is non-existent because it absolutely exists, just not as much as it used to say 50 years ago.

Since green is the color that matters in our capitalistic country, stop spending so much of your money (i.e. your life, because time is money) chasing expendable material items. If you work at a fast food spot making $8/hr, don't you know it will take almost 25 hours of your life to buy one pair of those expensive sneakers? ($8/hr X 25 hours = $200 gross; $200 gross - $40 taxes = $160). Don't you know some laborer in a Chinese factory slapped those shoes together in about 15 minutes? Did you even think about if that Chinese person was paid $15/hr for their time, the company can make a pair of those shoes for about $20? ($15/hr X 15 minutes = $3.75 labor; $3.75 labor + $16.25 material = $20). Do you see how silly and irresponsible it is to pay $160 for an item that only $16.25 of material and 15 minutes of time was put in to? Wake up! It's only worth $160 in your head, because you're using those shoes as a crutch to make yourself feel good.

Those who lack Knowledge of Self, try to create self-worth with material items. It won't work, because as soon as you get caught in a heavy rain with those shoes on, they're no longer fresh and your esteem takes the hit. You are not the first of our kind to make that mistake. Dr. Turner in *The Negro in Pennsylvania* noted "In 1797 it was said that a negress servant would wear a ball-dress worth many weeks' wages...and nearly the same criticism was repeated twenty-five years later."[160] The time has come for us to break this cycle! No crutch should be permanent. Release yourself and heal your soul, cultural self-esteem, sense of being, and sense of accomplishment with Knowledge of Self. Don't allow the capitalists to steal your time i.e. money from you. Live within your means at all times. If you want expensive material possessions, then the smart thing to do is invest the time necessary to increase your means! It is imperative that you allow the knowledge of your peoples' past accomplishments serve as the foundation of your self-esteem, not some leather, stitching, glue and a little logo. If you know your people spawned humanity, civilization, medicine, math, language, tools, etc. material items don't matter as much.

[160] Turner, 141.

Slaves With Swag

Turn off the video games, turn off the television, set aside all indulgent toxins and get to work! Don't be under the false impression that the bar Black people should aspire to is just above not being a slave. That game has been ran and re-ran. You see from the few examples in this book what we were capable of in the 1700 and 1800's! It's the 2000's now! Be a credit to your people. Contribute something to our society and our beloved Country. Make something, build something, DO SOMETHING! Be the producer the Creator intended you to be. And once you make it, reach back to those coming up behind you. Thank you for reading and feel free to contact me on Facebook, Twitter @AuthorDHinmon or via email at dth@knowledgeofselfpublishing.com. I look forwarding to hearing from you. Peace.[161]

---

[161] One final note. There is mention of quite a few prominent African Americans in this book. I want you to notice that none mentioned were entertainers or athletes. There is a very dangerous tendency to only speak of entertainers and athletes (Bill Cosby, Michael Jordan, etc.) when mentioning prominent or successful African Americans of the 21st century. The danger in that act is synonymizing popularity and riches with accomplishment. Ask any young Black boy what they want to be when they grow up and at least 75% will answer 'play in the NFL or NBA' without hesitation. Using athletes and entertainers exclusively as examples of Black accomplishment influences our young to only aspire to popularity and money through physical means instead of mental accomplishments. Since only a small percentage of humans possess the physical ability to perform at the highest levels, it leaves those who are good, but not good enough and those who have no physical skill at all clamoring for prosperous models to emulate. So, pay homage to and popularize your intellects, business people, doctors, lawyers, skilled laborers and political men and women of prominence to ensure the youth know those avenues are very much available to them and we are capable of much more than singing, dancing and playing ball. That is not meant to discount the feats of our athletes and entertainers because they are the very best at what they do. There just needs to be a healthy balance between the skill set of our children's role models.

Selected Bibliography

Aikin, John G. comp. *A Digest of the Laws of the State of Alabama: Containing All the Statutes of A Public and General Nature, in Force at the Close of the Session of the General Assembly, in January, 1833.* Philadelphia: Alexander Towar 19 St. James Street, 1833.

American Historical Society. *Annual Report of the American Historical Association for the Year 1903 vol. II.* Washington, D.C.: Government Printing Office, 1904.

Armistead, Wilson. *A Tribute for the Negro: Being a Vindication of the Moral, Intellectual, and Religious Capabilities of the Colored Portion of Mankind; With Particular Reference to the African Race.* Manchester, 1848, 309-12.

Atlee, Edwin P. MD. *An Address to the Citizens of Philadelphia, on the Subject of Slavery. Delivered on the 4th of 7th Month, (July,) A.D. 1833.* Philadelphia: 1833.

Ballagh, James Curtis A.B. *White Servitude in the Colony of Virginia. A Study of the System of Indentured Labor in the American Colonies.* Baltimore: Johns Hopkins Press, 1895.

Barber, John W. *A History of the Amistad Captives*, New Haven: E.L. & J.W. Barber, 1840.

Benezet, Anthony. *A Caution and Warning to Great Britain and Her Colonies, In a Short Representation of the Calamitous State of the Enslaved Negroes in the British Dominions. Collected from various Authors, and Submitted to the Serious CONSIDERATION of ALL, more specifically of THOSE in POWER.* Philadelphia: Printed by Henry Miller in Second Street, 1766.

Brackett, Jeffrey. *The Negro in Maryland, A Study of the Institution of Slavery.* Baltimore: Johns Hopkins University, 1889.

Carroll, Joseph Cephas. *Slave Insurrections in the United States, 1800-1865.* (Boston: Chapman & Grimes, 1938 : Mineola, NY: Dover Publications Inc, 2004).

Slaves With Swag

Coffin, Joshua. *An Account of Some of the Principal Slave Insurrections, and Others, Which Have Occurred, or Been Attempted, in the United States and Elsewhere, During the Last Two Centuries. With Various Remarks.* New York: American Anti-slavery Society, 1860.

Commons, John R. et. al. ed. *A Documentary History of American Industrial Society Vol. II.* Cleveland: Arthur H. Clark Co., 1910.

Corey, Charles H. *A History of the Richmond Theological Seminary, with Reminiscences of Thirty Years' Work Among Colored People of the South.* Richmond: J.W. Randolph Company, 1895.

Department of Commerce, Bureau of the Census. *Negro Population: 1790-1915.* Washington D.C.: Government Printing Office, 1918.

Digest of the Laws of the State of Alabama: Containing All the Statutes of A Public and General Nature, in Force at the Close of the Session of the General Assembly, in January, 1833. Compiled under the authority of the General Assembly by John G. Aikin. Philadelphia: Alexander Towar 19 St. James Street, 1833.

Equiano, Olaudah. *The Interesting Narrative of the Life of Olaudah Equiano or Gustavus Vassa, The African. Written By Himself.* 9th ed. London: Olaudah Equiano, 1789.

Gray, Thomas R. *The Confessions of Nat Turner, the Leader of the Late Insurrection in Southampton, VA. as Fully and Voluntarily Made to Thomas R. Gray...* Richmond: Thomas R. Gray, 1832.

Hamilton, James. *Negro Plot. An Account of the Late Intended Insurrection Among a Portion of the Blacks of the City of Charleston, South Carolina 2nd ed.* Boston: Joseph W. Ingraham, 1822. 17. Also available online as part of the University of North Carolina digitization project at http://docsouth.unc.edu/church/church/Hamilton/Hamilton.html.

Hewatt, Alexander. *An Historical Account of the Rise and Progress of the Colonies of South Carolina and Georgia, vol II.* London, 1779.

Holland, Edwin C., *A Refutation of The Calumnies Circulated Against The Southern & Western States, Respecting The Institution and Existence of Slavery Among Them. To Which is Added A Minute and Particular*

Selected Bibliography

Account of the Actual State and Condition of Their Negro Population Together With Historical Notices of all the Insurrections That Have Taken Place Since the Settlement of the Country. Charleston, S.C.: Printed By A.E. Miller, 1822.

Kelley, Edmond. *A Family Redeemed from Bondage; Being Rev. Edmond Kelley, (the Author,) His Wife, and Four Children.* New Bedford, MA: Edmond Kelley Publisher, 1851. Also available online as part of the University of North Carolina digitization project at http://docsouth.unc.edu/neh/kelley/kelley.html.

Marrs, Elijah. *Life and History of Rev. Elijah P. Marrs, First Pastor of Beargrass Baptist Church, and Author.* Louisville: Bradley & Gilbert Co., 1885. Also available online as part of the University of North Carolina digitization project at http://docsouth.unc.edu/neh/marrs/marrs.html.

Meachum, John Berry. *An Address to All the Colored Citizens of the United States.* Philadelphia: Printed by King and Baird, 1846.

Mott, Abigail. *Biographical Sketches and Interesting Anecdotes of Persons of Colour.* York: 1826.

Niles, H. & Son, ed. *Niles Weekly Register. Documents, Essays and Facts Together with Notices of the Arts and Manufacture, and a Record of the Events of the Times From September 1826, to March 1827- Vol. XXXI or, Volume VII-Third Series.* Baltimore: Franklin Press, 1827.

Pegues, A.W. *Our Baptist Ministers and Schools.* Springfield, MA: Wiley & Co., 1892.

Perry, Rev. Rufus L. *The Cushite or the Descendants of Ham as Found in the Sacred Scriptures and in the Writings of Ancient Historian and Poets From Noah to the Christian Era.* Springfield, MA: Wiley & Co., 1893

Rives, John C. *The Congressional Globe for the Second Session, Thirty-Second Congress: containing Speeches, Important Papers, Laws, etc.* New Series Vol. XXVII. Washington D.C.: Printed at the Office of John C. Rives, 1853.

Sandiford, Ralph. *Mystery of Iniquity in a Brief Examination of the Practice of the Times.* 2nd ed. Philadelphia, 1730.

Simmons, William J. *Men of Mark: Eminent, Progressive and Rising.* Cleveland: Geo. M. Rewell & Co., 1887

Slaves With Swag

Smith, Capt. J.S. *A Letter from Capt. J.S. Smith to the Revd. Mr. Hill on the State of the Negroe Slaves.* London: 1786.

Still, William. *Underground Railroad Records rev. ed.* Philadelphia: William Still Publisher, 1886.

Talbert, Horace. *The Sons of Allen: Together with a Sketch of the Rise and Progress of Wilberforce University, Wilberforce, Ohio.* Xenia, OH: The Aldine Press, 1906.

Tanner, Benjamin T. *An Apology For African Methodism.* Baltimore, 1867. Also available online as part of the University of North Carolina digitization project at http://docsouth.unc.edu/church/tanner/tanner.html.

Troy, Rev. William. *Hair-breadth Escapes from Slavery to Freedom.* Manchester, England: 1861.

Turner, Dr. Edward Raymond. *The Negro in Pennsylvania, Slavery – Servitude – Freedom, 1639-1861.* Washington, D.C.: American Historical Association, 1911.

Webb, William. *The History of William Webb, Composed by Himself.* Detroit: 1873.

White, J. Bliss comp. *Biography and Achievements of the Colored Citizens of Chattanooga,* 1904. Reprint, Signal Mountain, TN: Mountain Press, 2004.

Index

Slaves With Swag

Slaves With Swag